FAMOUS PERSONALITIES OF
FLIGHT
COOKBOOK

MARY HENDERSON

Published for the
National Air and Space Museum
by the
Smithsonian Institution Press
Washington, D.C.
1981

Library of Congress Cataloging in Publication Data

Henderson, Mary S
  Famous personalities of flight cookbook.

  Includes index.
  1. Cookery. 2. Aeronautics—Biography.
3. Astronautics—Biography. I. Title.
TX715.H513   641.5   80-20331
ISBN 0-87474-515-2

Photo Credits (by page numbers)

National Aeronautics and Space Administration: 14, 24, 30, 46, 80, 88, 89, 103, and 123; Yale University Library: 28; Charles Blair: 41; Ernest Gann: 52; Jimmy Dale Photo, Rancho Mirage, California: 55; United Press International: 64; Neta Snook Southern: 68; Institute of the Aeronautical Sciences: 75; Watson Photo for William C. Estler, conservator, Bonestell Space Art, Palo Alto, California: 99; *Naval Aviation News:* 108; Paul B. MacCready, Jr.: 116; Northrop Corporation: 119; and Dawson Ransome: 122.

CONTENTS

FOREWORD

When Mary Henderson told me she wanted to put together a cookbook based on the recipes of people who had spent their lives in aviation, or aerospace as it's now called, I said, "Sure, Mary, go ahead." But I thought to myself, "She'll never do it; those people didn't have their minds on cooking then, nor do they now." How wrong I was! How many must have come home from a long day at the wind tunnel or flight line, and submerged their frustrations in a stew pot, or celebrated their triumphs with a special dinner. Their flying records may have long since been broken, their accomplishments buried in the pages of a history book, but we can all duplicate and share with them a not-so-small part of their lives—the food they ate.

I can well remember my first day in orbit—eighteen hours of chasing Agenas and conducting scientific experiments, leaving me exhausted, but still exhilarated with one spectacular vista after another sweeping past my Gemini window. I was also famished, and reached into my supply locker for something to eat. Not much there, you may say, just a flattened tube of dehydrated cream of chicken soup. But after adding some warm water, it turned to ambrosia, and never again can I eat cream of chicken soup without thinking of the green isle of Formosa glistening in the sunlight below me, or the California coastline rushing up at great speed.

I have not given the recipe for this soup, because I don't have it, as it was concocted by some government wizard. But I have included a mainstay of the Collins family, a lamb curry which has seen us through good and bad times, adding an extra sheen to the one and taking a few rough edges off the other. I'm delighted that, in this small volume, many of my good friends have done likewise. It's nice to be able to share even a tiny part of their highly unusual lives. Thanks, Mary, you were right.

Michael Collins

ACKNOWLEDGMENTS

The concept for this book grew out of a desire to know more about those who have, in one way or another, contributed to the story of flight. Since cooking is a personal means of expression, I am convinced that knowing someone's favorite recipe provides an insight into his or her personality. A cookbook seemed to be a fascinating way to learn more about people and their flying machines. I hope that you will enjoy reading and using this book as much as I have enjoyed accumulating the recipes and putting them together.

I would like to thank Michael Collins, who, while director of the National Air and Space Museum, gave his approval to this project and has since continued to be encouraging and helpful. James Dean, former curator of art, was a staunch supporter during the seemingly endless era of recipe testing and research. Special thanks go to Donald Lopez, department chairman for aeronautics, and curators Claudia Oakes and Thomas Crouch, for letting me badger them with questions, and for giving excellent counsel and advice. Without the aid of Librarian Catherine D. Scott and Public Relations Officer Rita Bobowski this book would not have been possible. Carol Hodges, independent food consultant, and Royal Frey, curator of the Air Force Museum, kindly consented to review the manuscript, and their comments and suggestions have been enormously helpful.

This book is dedicated to all of those people who have so kindly contributed their recipes, and thus a small part of themselves.

PIONEERS

Neil A. Armstrong
Preserving Children

Bernt Balchen
Whole Poached Salmon
Fillet of Beef

Octave A. Chanute
Scallops with Mushrooms
Requested Liver

James H. Doolittle
Vichyssoise

Amelia Earhart
Sour Cream Waffles

John H. Glenn, Jr.
Annie Glenn's Ham Loaf

Robert H. Goddard
Ranch Spaghetti
Date and Nut Pudding
Snow Sauce

Charles A. Lindbergh
Swedish Party Cakes
Oatmeal Cookies

Wernher Von Braun
German Nut Cake

Leigh Wade
Mu-Hsu

Wilbur and Orville Wright
Pear Salad
Mayonnaise
Carrie's Christmas Mold

Charles Yeager
Cornbread Sticks

Neil Armstrong waves to well-wishers as the Apollo 11 crew pre-pares for the launch of the first lunar-landing mission.

Neil A. Armstrong

As commander of the Apollo 11 moon-landing mission, Neil Armstrong became the first human being to set foot on another celestial body at 10:56 P.M. EDT on July 20, 1969. A highly qualified test pilot, he had also performed the first successful docking of two vehicles in space during the Gemini 8 mission. During this earth orbital flight, his quick reactions brought the spacecraft to a safe landing when it unexplainedly began to spin out of control. His passion for flight had developed early in his life—he had a pilot's license before he was old enough to drive a car and built a wind tunnel in the basement to study aerodynamics. After the historic moon landing, Armstrong served for a short period as deputy associate administrator for aeronautics at the headquarters of the National Aeronautics and Space Administration in Washington. He went to the University of Cincinnati in 1971 as associate director of the Institute for Applied Interdisciplinary Research. In 1980, he joined Cardwell International, a manufacturer of oil drilling equipment. *Comment from Neil A. Armstrong*

Preserving Children

6 children
3 dogs (at least)
1 large grassy field
flowers
narrow strip of brook with pebbles
deep blue sky
hot sun

Mary Teichgraeber is my aunt and has given permission to quote this recipe.

• Mix the children with the dogs and empty into the field, stirring constantly. Sprinkle the field with flowers. Pour brook gently over the pebbles. Cover all with a deep blue sky and bake in the hot sun. When the children are well browned, they may be removed. Will be found just right for setting away to cool in the bathtub.

Bernt Balchen
1899–1973

A pioneer and innovator in the conquest of the Arctic, Norwegian–American Bernt Balchen piloted a Ford 4AT Tri-motor on the first flight over the South Pole in November 1929 for Comdr. Richard E. Byrd. By sacrificing food supplies to lighten the plane, he gained enough altitude to fly over the mountainous "hump" which barricaded the polar plateau. Balchen was made an Air Force colonel during World War II; because of his expertise in Arctic flight, he flew numerous missions to assist patriots in occupied Norway. He later commanded many dramatic rescue missions from Greenland. *Recipes and comments from Mrs. Bernt Balchen*

Bernt loved to cook and wrote a cookbook which was published in Norway. These were two of his favorites, even though they were cooked inside, in the kitchen! Whenever possible he cooked on the outdoor grill.

Whole Poached Salmon

Serves 4

1 bottle dry white wine, or 1 quart water
½ cup wine vinegar
1 tablespoon salt
3 cloves
1 teaspoon freshly ground pepper
1 bay leaf

3 garlic cloves
1 small onion
⅓ cup carrot, chopped
spring of parsley or dill
dash of thyme
1 to 2 pounds salmon, cleaned but left whole

• Mix all ingredients except salmon and boil about 10 or 15 minutes. Adjust seasonings to taste. Cool. • Use a rack large enough to hold the entire fish, and a pan large enough to hold them both. Lay the fish on the rack, place rack in pan, and pour the broth over the fish. Cover pan with lid or foil and place in preheated 375° oven. Cook for about 15 minutes per pound of fish, or until it flakes easily, checking halfway through the cooking time and skimming broth if necessary. • Serve hot with Hollandaise or white-wine sauce, boiled potatoes, and salad. If served cold, allow salmon to cool in the stock, which will jell. Garnish with lemon or tomato wedges, sliced cucumber, and mayonnaise, rémoulade, or tartar sauce.

Fillet of Beef

Serves 4

1½-pound whole fillet of beef

3 slices lean bacon, cut in small pieces

1 truffle, diced

1 cup Marsala wine

1½ ounces Cognac

¼ teaspoon salt

⅛ teaspoon freshly ground pepper

1 stalk celery, minced

3½ teaspoons parsley, chopped

2 tablespoons butter

1 medium onion, chopped

1 carrot, diced

½ cup beef stock or consommé

1 tablespoon flour

• Lard the fillet by making cuts in the meat with a thin sharp knife and inserting in each cut 1 piece of bacon and 1 piece of truffle. Tie meat with string to hold the shape. • Place in a deep dish and pour in the Marsala wine and Cognac. Add salt, pepper, ½ of the celery, and ½ teaspoon of the parsley. Marinate for 2 hours, turning frequently. • Remove from marinade. Place meat in a deep frying pan or Dutch oven with 1 tablespoon butter, the onion, carrot, and remaining celery and parsley. Brown the meat thoroughly on all sides over medium heat. When brown, add the marinade and beef stock; cover and cook for 20 minutes (meat should be medium-rare at this point). Remove from pan. • Remove liquid from pan and reserve. Melt remaining butter and add flour, stirring until foamy. Return liquid to pan, slowly, stirring constantly. Cook until slightly thickened. Slice meat and serve with this gravy.

Octave A. Chanute

1832–1910

A famous civil engineer, Octave Chanute became captivated by the attempts of others to glide and to achieve powered flight. He became a devoted student of aeronautical history and in 1894 his book *Progress in Flying Machines* helped to popularize aviation research. He organized and gave financial support to aeronautical activities at the turn of the century, and his encouragement of the Wright brothers was a significant factor in their success. *Recipes from Mr. and Mrs. Octave A. Chanute III*

Scallops with Mushrooms   Serves 4

1 pound scallops
3 ounces butter
½ pound mushrooms, sliced
3 stalks celery, diced
½ small onion, grated
½ green pepper, minced

⅛ teaspoon basil
2 cups basic white sauce
½ cup cracker crumbs
4 teaspoons grated Cheddar cheese
parsley sprigs

• Wash and wipe scallops with a damp cloth; set aside. • Melt 2 ounces of the butter in a saucepan over medium flame. Add mushrooms, celery, onion, green pepper, and basil; simmer gently for 10 minutes, or until celery and mushrooms are tender but not soft. Remove from heat. • Prepare any basic white sauce of your choice. • Add scallops to the mushroom mixture, and heat for 5 minutes. Add the white sauce and mix well. Pour into casserole and cover with cracker crumbs. Sprinkle over cheese and dot with the remaining butter. • Bake in a preheated oven at 350° for 25 minutes, or until golden brown. Garnish with parsley sprigs.

Requested Liver   Serves 6

6 slices bacon
1½ pounds baby beef liver, cut into serving-size pieces
all-purpose flour
1 large onion, sliced
1 medium-size green pepper, seeded and sliced
1 envelope dry onion-soup mix (enough for 4–6 servings)
1 pound can stewed tomatoes
seasoning salt
pepper

• In a wide frying pan over medium heat, fry bacon until crisp. Set bacon aside on paper towels to drain. Pour off and reserve bacon drippings, returning 2 tablespoons to the pan. • Dredge liver in the flour, shake off excess. Fry liver just until lightly browned on both sides, adding more drippings to the pan as needed. Arrange liver in a 9 × 13-inch baking dish. • Add onion and green pepper to the frying pan and cook until onion is limp. Spoon vegetables evenly over liver, then sprinkle with onion-soup mix. Pour tomatoes over all, sprinkle with seasoning salt and pepper, and top with bacon. • Cover and bake in a 350° oven for 25 minutes.

James H. Doolittle

World War II hero, air racer, and test pilot—Jimmy Doolittle's career has spanned five decades of aviation history. He pioneered "blind flying," was in the forefront of the development of 100-octane fuel, led the Tokyo Raid in 1942, and set many speed and distance records. He commanded the United States 8th Air Force in England during World War II. General Doolittle is currently a member of the Board of Directors of Mutual of Omaha. *Comments and recipe from James H. Doolittle*

Vichyssoise   Serves 6

Although I hew wood, carry water, and wash dishes, I do not cook and depend entirely upon my favorite girl Joe (my wife) where the preparation of food is concerned. This is one of her specialities which I particularly enjoy.

4 or 5 leeks and 1 white onion, sliced thin (or 2 white onions)
3 tablespoons butter or margarine
4 cups chicken broth
4 medium-size potatoes
1 stalk celery
1 cup cream or milk
salt and pepper to taste
chopped chives

• Sauté leeks and onion slices in butter or margarine until transparent. • Add chicken broth, potatoes, and celery. Cook until vegetables are tender. Cool. • Put mixture in blender in batches and blend until smooth. Just before serving stir in the cream or milk and salt and pepper. • Serve cold, topped with chopped chives.

James Doolittle and the Vought 02U Corsair during his blind-flight training at Mitchell Field, New York, in 1929.

Amelia Earhart

1898–1937

Although she was the first woman to fly the Atlantic as a passenger in 1928, Amelia Earhart determined to prove that she could be the first woman to make the trip solo. She achieved this objective in May 1932 in a single-engine Lockheed Vega. Not content with establishing this new record, Amelia Earhart went on to become the first person to fly solo across the Pacific from Hawaii to California. In 1937 in an attempt to circumnavigate the globe, she disappeared in the Pacific. A spokeswoman for the cause of women in aviation throughout her brief career, she continues to be an inspiration to women today. *Recipe from unidentified newspaper clipping*

Ms. Earhart, commenting on "in flight" meals during her career: *What to feed a football team or how to plan meals for a crew—these things are well known. But there has been little intelligent research on what to feed a pilot, who has to sit still for as long as thirty hours sometimes, and must maintain the utmost mental concentration.—* Unidentified newspaper clipping.

Sour Cream Waffles   Makes 5

2 cups sifted flour
1 teaspoon baking soda
½ teaspoon salt
1 tablespoon sugar
2 eggs, separated
2 cups sour cream

• Sift together flour, soda, salt, and sugar. Mix together well. • Beat egg yolks until light. Combine with cream. Add to dry ingredients, beating until smooth. • Beat egg whites until stiff; gently fold into batter. • Bake on a waffle iron according to the directions provided by the manufacturer.

Of her solo trans-Atlantic flight; she wrote: *I didn't bother much about food for myself. The really important thing was fuel for the engine. It drank more than 300 gallons of gasoline. My own trans-Atlantic rations consisted of one can of tomato juice which I punctured and sipped through a straw.*—From *The Fun of It* by Amelia Earhart (New York: Brewer, Warren, and Putnam, 1932), p. 217.

Amelia Earhart climbing into her Lockheed Vega.

John H. Glenn, Jr.

John Glenn poses in front of the Friendship 7 *spacecraft.*

In 1962 John Glenn became the first American to orbit the earth, in the Mercury-Atlas *Friendship 7.* This significant flight demonstrated that it was important to send a man rather than a machine into space to deal with the unforeseen problems of travel outside the earth's atmosphere. He later assisted in the Project Apollo planning, specializing in the design and development of the spacecraft and flight control systems. In 1964 he joined the Royal Crown Cola Company and entered politics; in 1974 he was elected senator from the state of Ohio. *Recipe from Mrs. John H. Glenn, Jr.*

Annie Glenn's Ham Loaf   Serves 6

1 pound cured ham, chopped
½ pound fresh ham, chopped
1½ cups dry bread crumbs
2 eggs
¾ cup milk
pepper
¼ cup sugar
¼ cup water
¼ cup vinegar
1 tablespoon mustard

• Mix ham, bread crumbs, eggs, milk, and pepper well and form into a loaf. • Heat sugar with water and vinegar until sugar dissolves. Add mustard. • Pour mustard sauce over loaf, and bake at 350° for 1½ hours. Baste loaf several times during baking (sauce will be syrupy).

Robert H. Goddard

1882–1945

Despite jocular criticism of his work, such as a newspaper headline reading "Moon Rocket Misses Target by 238,799½ Miles," Robert Goddard persevered in his research and experiments with rockets. His 1919 book, *A Method of Reaching Extreme Altitudes,* provided one of the first well-reasoned mathematical proofs of the possibility of space flight. A professor of physics at Clark University, he launched the world's first liquid propellant rocket from a Massachusetts cabbage patch in 1926. Over the next two decades he worked tirelessly to develop improved rocket engines and other devices to make travel outside the atmosphere possible. Although space flight remained little more than a pipe dream during his lifetime, Goddard never lost faith, for as he remarked, "The dream of yesterday is the hope of today and the reality of tomorrow."* *Recipes from* Favorite Foods of Famous People, A. O. Negrotto (New Orleans: Hope Publications, 1971).

Ranch Spaghetti   Serves 6

½ pound spaghetti
¼ cup butter
½ to 1 pound lean round steak, ground
1½ green peppers, finely chopped
1½ onions, finely chopped
1 can mushrooms
1 medium can tomatoes
salt and pepper to taste
½ pound cheese, grated

• Cook spaghetti according to package directions. • Melt butter in a saucepan; add meat and brown over medium heat. Stir in peppers and onions, and cook until soft. • Add mushrooms and their juice and the tomatoes; simmer for about 20 minutes over low heat. • Toss with drained noodles and half of the cheese. Add salt and pepper to taste. Transfer to a baking pan, top with remaining cheese, and bake at 350° for approximately 15 minutes or until cheese is melted and brown.

*From the *Papers of Robert Goddard,* edited by Esther C. Goddard (New York: McGraw-Hill, 1970), vol 1, p. 66.

Date and Nut Pudding   Serves 4

2½ tablespoons butter
⅔ cup sugar
2 eggs
2 tablespoons flour
⅓ teaspoon baking powder
⅔ cup milk
⅔ cup dates, chopped
½ cup walnuts, chopped

● Cream butter with the sugar. Add eggs one at a time, beating well after each addition. ● Mix flour with baking powder; add, with milk, to the batter. Stir in the dates and nuts. ● Bake in a well-greased dish at 325° for about 45 minutes. Serve hot with Snow Sauce or whipped cream.

Snow Sauce
2 tablespoons butter
1 cup powdered sugar
1 egg
pinch of salt
1 teaspoon vanilla or sherry wine
¾ cup whipping cream

● Cream together butter, sugar, and egg until smooth. Add salt and vanilla or wine. ● Whip cream until stiff. Fold into creamed mixture.

Charles A. Lindbergh
1902–1974

Lindbergh remains one of the most famous heroes in the history of aviation. His popularity is based not only on the fact that he was the first to solo nonstop from New York to Paris in 1927 in the *Spirit of St. Louis,* but also on his independent personality. His decision to fly alone, to discard a radio and even a parachute to save weight, to navigate by dead-reckoning, and his use of a relatively inexpensive plane built by a small firm (partially with his personal savings), all captured the public imagination at the time and still do today. His work in aeronautics after his historic flight helped shape the growth of that industry, and during World War II he aided in the development of military aircraft. In peacetime, he directed his concern to the problems of the environment. Of the future, he once said: "Following the paths of science we become constantly more aware of mysteries beyond scientific research . . . the great adventures of the future lie in voyages inconceivable by our 20th-century rationality—beyond the solar system, through distant galaxies, possibly through peripheries untouched by time and space."*   *Recipes and comments from the Minnesota Historical Society*

*Charles A. Lindbergh, *Autobiography of Values,* ed. by William Jovanovich; co-editor, Judith A. Schiff (New York: Harcourt Brace Jovanovich, 1978), p. 357.

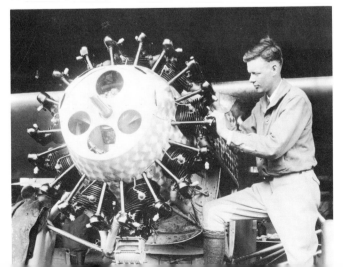

Charles Lindbergh examines the engine of the Spirit of St. Louis.

Swedish Party Cakes
Makes approximately 100 small cookies

My mother often made a Swedish butter cookie— very rich, yellow, and in the form of an 'O.' This was my favorite cookie.

1 pound butter
1 scant cup sugar
1 egg
3 to 4 cups flour
2 scant teaspoons baking powder
1 teaspoon lemon or almond extract

• Remove butter from refrigerator to soften. Cream with sugar until light and fluffy. • Beat in egg thoroughly. Add 3 cups of flour and mix well; add more flour if needed to make a dough which holds its shape, yet is soft. Mix in baking powder and extract. • Force through a pastry tube onto an ungreased cookie sheet forming the cookies into ring shapes or roll into little balls and flatten. Bake at 350° for about 8 to 10 minutes or until a deep lemon yellow in color.

Oatmeal Cookies   Makes approximately 100 cookies

2 cups flour	2 eggs
½ teaspoon salt	4 tablespoons milk
¾ teaspoon soda	2 cups regular rolled oats
1 teaspoon cinnamon	1 cup raisins
1 cup butter or margarine	½ cup cherries, chopped
1 cup sugar	½ cup nuts, chopped

• Sift flour together with salt, soda, and cinnamon.
• Cream butter or margarine with sugar until light and fluffy. Beat in eggs, one at a time. • Stir in the flour mixture alternately with the milk; then add the oats, raisins, cherries, and nuts. • Drop by teaspoonfuls on buttered cookie tins and bake at 350° for 15 to 20 minutes or until golden brown.

Charles Lindbergh and his mother, about 1908.

28

Wernher Von Braun
1912-1977

Only thirty-three years old when he and his key associates surrendered to the United States Army at the end of World War II, Wernher Von Braun was already the world's most experienced and successful rocket engineer. He had served as technical director for the German rocket research facility at Peenemünde, guiding the development of the V-2, a weapon that also served as a major stepping stone on the road to space flight. After coming to the United States, he became a spokesman for an increased space effort. He served as technical advisor and project director on the United States Army rocket programs and as chief of guided-missile development at the Redstone Arsenal in Alabama. In 1956 he became director of the Army's Ballistic Missile Agency. When it became part of the National Aeronautics and Space Administration in 1960 as the Marshall Space Flight Center, Von Braun was selected as its director. He was responsible for developing the family of rockets that carried the first United States satellite into orbit and later boosted the Apollo astronauts to the moon.
Recipe from Mrs. Wernher Von Braun

German Nut Cake   Serves 6

Cake
8 eggs, separated
½ teaspoon cream of tartar
½ cup sugar
2 or 3 tablespoons rum or brandy
1½ cups grated pecans

• Preheat over to 325°. Grease and flour two 9-inch round layer pans. • Beat egg whites until foamy; add cream of tartar and beat until stiff peaks form. • In a separate bowl, beat egg yolks with sugar until light. Stir in rum or brandy. • Pour egg yolk mixture over egg whites, and sprinkle nuts on top. Fold together gently but thoroughly. Pour into pans and bake 1 hour. Cool in pans before removing to add icing.

Wernher Von Braun and the Saturn V rocket.

Icing
1½ cups confectioners sugar
3 tablespoons hot water
2 tablespoons lemon juice
½ cup pecan halves

● Mix sugar with hot water; add lemon juice. Blend well (this icing will be rather thin). ● Drizzle half of icing evenly over bottom layer, covering completely. Add second layer and coat top, allowing icing to run down sides. Garnish with pecan halves.

Leigh Wade

Honored in the Aviation Hall of Fame and recipient of the distinguished Mackay Trophy, Leigh Wade was an army flier in World War I. He was one of eight pilots selected to fly four planes in 1924 from Seattle in an attempt to make the first circumnavigation of the world by air. With frequent stops to refuel the open-cockpit Douglas World Cruisers, the fliers accomplished an incredible feat despite the lack of navigational aids, weather forecasting, and radio communication, and the relatively primitive state of the art of aircraft and engine technology. Unfortunately, eighty miles north of the Faeroe Islands en route to Iceland engine trouble caused Wade's plane to make a forced landing in the North Atlantic Ocean where the two pilots were rescued; however, two of the planes completed the trip and returned to Seattle. Wade continued his army career, ultimately retiring from his position as chief of the air section of the Joint Brazil/United States Military Mission. *Recipe from Leigh Wade*

Mu-Hsu

Serves 4

4 large pork chops (or an equivalent quantity of chicken, beef, or fresh hamburger)
2 tablespoons cooking oil
5 large onions, chopped
2 green peppers
1 pound mushrooms, cleaned and sliced
¼ teaspoon minced garlic
2 pounds of bean sprouts
1 small bunch of celery, chopped
1½ bunches of parsley, minced
4 beef bouillon cubes, crushed
3 or 4 cubes or sticks of candied ginger
pinch of salt and a dash of pepper
1 can water chestnuts

• Brown chops or other meat in a wok or large frying pan. Reduce heat to low and cook to desired doneness. Set aside. • Add cooking oil to a pan and stir-fry the onions, green peppers, and mushrooms until cooked but slightly crunchy. • Stir in other ingredients and cook until done to taste. Return meat to pan and stir a few more minutes until heated. • Serve over rice; add soy sauce to taste.

Wilbur Wright

1867–1912

Orville Wright

1871–1948

Wilbur, Orville, and Katharine Wright with President William Howard Taft.

Behind the calm and unassuming manner of two Ohio bicycle makers lay brilliant minds. In only four short years the Wright brothers cut through a morass of speculation and guesswork to solve the problem of powered flight. They began with careful observations of birds and a close examination of the pitfalls that had trapped other experimenters. They then continued with a systematic approach to solving aerodynamics using a series of manned gliders and a homemade wind tunnel. Their persistance and careful research enabled them to succeed where others had failed and culminated in 1903 with the first workable airplane—and the inauguration of the air age. *Recipes and comments from Mrs. Ivonette Wright Miller, niece of the Wright brothers.*

Mrs. Ivonette Wright Miller, niece of the Wright brothers, says of her uncles:
"Orville and Wilbur were both good cooks. They were particular about their food, and had definite ways of doing things.

"Orville usually made the fudge or caramel candy for his nieces and nephews when they visited on Sunday afternoons. In later years when he was summering at his island in Georgian Bay, he made orange marmalade for the children visiting him there, using his long thermometer to be sure it had boiled enough. It disappeared so quickly that he could hardly keep the supply coming fast enough.

He made delicious blueberry pie, using berries picked on the island. Carrie Grumbach, who had come to work for them when she was only 14 years old, had given him instructions about how to make good crust. Carrie served them well and with great devotion for 46 years. When the Wrights were at Kitty Hawk, Orville made biscuits without milk or eggs, and they were said to be very tasty.

Uncle Will liked to stuff the turkey at Christmas and Thanksgiving time. He always made a ceremony of it. He set out the ingredients just so, before starting, rubbing his hands together like a magician about to perform one of his most exacting tricks, measuring the bird with a shrewd appraising eye, and then always declaiming dramatically, 'Ah, but 'tis a fine beast!' Wilbur taught Carrie how to make gravy. He happened to be in the kitchen when she was having difficulty, and he said, 'Now Carrie, let's dump this out and start all over.' He went through it step by step, and it came out about perfect. In later years, when anyone told Carrie how delicious the gravy was, she always said, 'I ought to be able to make it well, Mr. Will taught me how.' "

Pear Salad   Serves 12-16

This was one of Uncle Orville's favorite salads. We still serve it at Christmas time, because of the happy memories it brings back, and because it is traditional.

1 large can pineapple juice (1 quart, 14 ounces)
3 envelopes gelatin
1 cup water
½ cup sugar
pinch of salt
1 teaspoon lemon juice

1 teaspoon vinegar
2 cans pears, drained (small pears are best)
8 ounces cream cheese
onion juice
pimiento and green pepper strips
lettuce

• Strain pineapple juice through cheese cloth, several times if necessary, until clear. • Heat the juice to a boil. Soften the gelatin in the water, and dissolve it in the juice. Add sugar, salt, lemon juice, and vinegar. • Pour one-half of the juice mixture into a 12-cup-capacity ring mold and let stand for approximately ½ hour or until slightly jelled. Keep the other half of the juice mixture in a cool, but not cold, place. • Mix the cream cheese with a few drops of onion juice, and stuff the pears with this mixture. Decorate with pimientos and green pepper strips. When the juice in the ring mold is jelled enough to hold the pears, turn the pears decorated side down and press slightly into the gelatin. Return to the refrigerator until firm, then add the remainder of the juice mixture. • Chill until set. Turn out on a platter and surround with lettuce. Place a small bowl of mayonnaise in the center of the ring and arrange small pieces of lettuce around the edge of the bowl.

Mayonnaise   Makes approximately 2 cups

1 tablespoon flour
1 tablespoon olive oil
dry mustard
⅓ cup boiling water
1 egg yolk
1 cup olive oil
juice of ½ lemon
powdered sugar
salt

• Mix flour, olive oil, a pinch of dry mustard, and the boiling water together. Cook over low heat, stirring constantly, until smooth and slightly thickened. Cool. • Turn into mixing bowl and add the egg yolk. Beating on high speed, add the oil a few drops at a time, alternating with lemon juice. Beat until thickened. • Add sugar and salt to taste.

Carrie's Christmas Mold   Serves 14-16

Fig Ice Cream
1 cup sugar
milk
4 mashed figs or 16 crumbled macaroons
vanilla
1 quart cream

This is what we looked forward to every Christmas eve for family dinner at Hawthorn Hill, when from ten to sixteen of us gathered to celebrate. Sometimes Carrie would change the fig mixture and use crumbled macaroons. It was scrumptious! We always hoped that when Carrie served us, it would be one of the bigger slices.

She always made her ice cream in the old-fashioned freezer that had to be cranked, then packed in salted ice. Today, one could buy the ice cream; however, nothing could equal the tasteful goodness of the homemade variety. The memory of the real thing will never be forgotten.

• Mix sugar with enough milk to moisten. • If using figs, cook until tender in a minimum of water; add sugar and stir over medium heat until sugar is dissolved and mixture is thick. If using macaroons, stir sugar over high heat until dissolved; add macaroons. • Add vanilla to taste and cool. • Add the cream and place in freezer. Remove after 45 minutes and beat with an electric mixer. Return to freezer for ½ hour and remove and beat again; repeat twice to break down ice crystals and create a lighter ice cream. Mixture may also be frozen in an ice-cream freezer.

Chocolate Ice Cream
1 cup sugar (more if desired)
milk
2 squares unsweetened chocolate, melted
vanilla
1 quart cream

• Mix sugar with enough milk to moisten; add melted chocolate. Stir over medium heat until smooth and thick. • Add vanilla to taste and cool. • Add the cream and process according to directions for fig ice cream.

To Mold
• Line a ½ gallon melon mold or bowl with the chocolate mixture to a 1-inch thickness, making a hollow center. Fill with the fig or macaroon ice cream. • Place in freezer and when ready to serve, remove from mold and decorate with maraschino cherries. Cut portions with a warm knife.

Charles Yeager

Charles Yeager (right) consults with Lawrence Bell during testing of the Bell X-1A.

In October 1947 Chuck Yeager became the first to fly faster than the speed of sound in the Bell X-1, breaking the sound barrier and opening the way to further developments in supersonic flight. He had been a World War II ace, shooting down thirteen enemy aircraft, including one of Germany's first jet fighters. Several years after his historic flight, he was appointed commander of the Air Force Test Pilot School. He retired in 1975 as a brigadier general and now lives in Cedar Ridge, California. *Recipe and comments from Charles Yeager*

Mom Yeager made these cornsticks for me when I was growing up in West Virginia. They are really good with butter and sorghum.

Cornbread Sticks   Makes 14

1 cup white cornmeal
1 tablespoon flour
1 scant teaspoon salt
¼ teaspoon soda
2 tablespoons bacon fat
buttermilk

• Mix dry ingredients together. Add 1 tablespoon bacon fat and stir in buttermilk, a tablespoon at a time, until the mixture is moistened and smooth, but not too liquid. • Put a few drops of the remaining bacon fat in the bottom of each cornbread-stick pan. Place pan in a 450° oven until the fat sizzles. Then spoon cornbread mix into pan until ⅔ full. • Bake in a 450° oven for 3 to 5 minutes or until brown. Remove from oven and immediately turn cornsticks upside down in the pan so that they will remain crisp.

FLIERS

Marian Banks
Steak with Pea Pods
Flying Chicken

Charles F. Blair
Tuna Fish

Kay A. Brick
Chicken à l'Asparagus
Brick Beef Stew

Claire Lee Chennault
Oriental Salad
Concubine Delight

Jacqueline Cochran
Popinosh
Pecan Pie

A. Scott Crossfield
Dry Martini

Betty Skelton Frankman
Tonga Tabu Grill
Snow Cake

Royal D. Frey
AAF POW's Delight

Ernest K. Gann
Gann's Cheese Fondue

George H. Gay
Tessie's Goulash

Barry M. Goldwater
Navajo Fry Bread

Clifford W. Henderson
Henderson's Hot Buttered Rum

Beverly Howard
Upside-down Cake

Benjamin S. Kelsey
Benjamin's Brownies
Steak Teriyaki

Henry T. Merrill
Air Mail Meatloaf
Eggs à la Merrill

Jerrie Mock
Bastilia
Couscous

Jeanette Piccard
Kidney and Mushrooms

Elwood Quesada
Coffee Ice Cream Supreme

Cliff Robertson
Spaghetti Vongole

Neta Snook Southern
Bread and Butter Pickles

Carl Andrew Spaatz
White Gazpacho

Louise M. Thaden
Quiche Lorraine

Roscoe Turner
Sweet Potato Pie

Fay Gillis Wells
Sweet and Sour Stuffed Cabbage Rolls

Robert M. White
Party Paté

Alford J. Williams, Jr.
Orange-glazed Pork Chops
Green Pea and Bean Salad
Pumpkin Bread

Steve Wittman
Green Bean Baked Dish
Sugar Cookies

Marian Banks

Marian Banks is the first and only grandmother to win the Powder Puff Derby which she did in 1972 in her Piper Comanche 260. The 2,616-mile transcontinental race started from San Carlos, California, and ended at Toms River, New Jersey. As well as racing in seventeen of the derbies, the perky and versatile Ms. Banks is chairman of the board of the All-Women's Transcontinental Air Race, Inc. She has received one of aviation's highest awards, the Paul Tissandier Diploma of the Fédération Aéronautique Internationale in 1978. *Recipes from Marian Banks*

"She's not content with thinking old thoughts,
Of resting, retiring, or dying
Don't bring Grandma your mending to do,
For Grandma has taken up flying."

Excerpt from a poem by an anonymous writer, adapted by Peg Axtell for the *Powder Puff Derby: Update 1974-1977 and Flash Backs* (1979), a commemorative album.

Steak with Pea Pods   Serves 4

¾ pound sirloin steak or other broiling cut
¾ cup soy sauce
¼ cup sherry
2 tablespoons sugar
1 teaspoon grated fresh ginger or ⅓ teaspoon ground ginger

1 clove garlic grated or ⅛ teaspoon garlic powder
3 tablespoons oil
1 large onion, sliced
1 can water chestnuts, sliced
1 package frozen pea pods
1 tablespoon cornstarch

• Slice the steak thinly, against the grain of the meat. Cut into bite-size pieces. • Mix the soy sauce, sherry, sugar, ginger, and garlic together. Place steak in this marinade for 1 hour. • Cook onion in oil over high heat for a few minutes, until almost cooked through. Reserving marinade, add steak and stir over heat until brown. Mix in water chestnuts and pea pods. • Mix the cornstarch into the marinade. Pour over the steak and vegetables and cook until the sauce is thick. • Serve at once over wild or regular rice. Accompany this with a mandarin-orange salad.

Flying Chicken   Serves 4

8 tortillas, cut into eights
1 frying chicken, cut into
  parts
flour
salt
pepper
cooking oil
1 can chili sauce
1 can cream of chicken soup
⅓ cup water or Sauterne
1 pint sour cream
⅓ pound mushrooms,
  sliced
1 package frozen green
  peas (optional)
1 small jar pimientos
  (optional)

• Dust chicken parts with flour, salt, and pepper. Brown over medium heat in a small amount of oil. • Reserve tortillas. • Mix remaining ingredients well to form a sauce. • Line a greased casserole dish with half of the tortillas and add half of the chicken and sauce. Repeat. Refrigerate for several hours or overnight so that the tortillas soak up some of the liquid. • Bake at 350° for approximately 45 minutes. Serve with taco sauce, if desired.

Charles F. Blair

1909–1978

Charles Blair and his wife, Maureen O'Hara.

Although the North pole had been crossed many times by large military planes, Charles Blair determined to be the first to make the trip solo in 1951. Modifying a 1943 army-surplus Mustang for the long-distance haul, he made the trip not by the complex navigational devices previously used, but by tracking the sun. This method of navigation and careful planning enabled him to make the crossing in well under eleven hours, flying so fast that he beat the sun from Norway to Alaska. In 1959, as a brigadier general, he led Operation Julius Caesar, the first flight of jet fighters to follow this route. Charles Blair was also an authority on flying boats, and owned and operated Antilles Air Boats of the Virgin Islands.

I must confess to be somewhat less than brilliant in this field of endeavor, in spite of the fact that I did get the cooking merit badge when I was a Boy Scout. Since that time my skills have lapsed to the point that my only remaining capability is the skillful boiling of an occasional egg. I do have a special recipe for breakfast which is half a can of tuna fish mixed with a dash of mayonnaise. Have been consuming this for years without suffering excessive brain damage from the consumption of mercury alleged to be heavily resident in it. Incidentally, my wife joins me in consuming the other half of the can. Perhaps this tuna fish habit has been a source of strength to me, much like spinach was to Popeye the Sailor Man.—Letter from General Blair dated August 4, 1977.

Kay A. Brick

A squadron commander of the Women's Airforce Service Pilots during World War II, Kay Brick has also ferried aircraft from Alaska to Australia, and flown to Cuba with her mother in the rear cockpit. She has been for over thirty-three years a member of the "99's," a group of women pilots organized by Amelia Earhart in 1929. This group sponsored the first All-Women Transcontinental Air Race which came to be known as the "Powder Puff Derby" held from 1947 to 1976. Among many awards, she received the Paul Tissandier Diploma of the Fédération Aéronautique Internationale in 1972. *Recipes from Kay Brick*

Chicken à l'Asparagus   Serves 4

1 pound asparagus, fresh or frozen
1 can cream of mushroom soup
1 cup sliced mushrooms
pepper
2 to 4 chicken breasts, cooked and sliced (dark meat or turkey may be substituted)

⅓ cup dried bread crumbs
2 tablespoons parsley, fresh or dried
3 tablespoons slivered almonds
3 tablespoons melted butter or margarine

• Cook asparagus in boiling, lightly salted water until tender. Drain. • Warm soup, thinning slightly with water; add mushrooms and a dash of pepper. • Place chicken pieces in the bottom of a baking dish about 6 × 10 × 1½ inches in size. Spoon half of soup over chicken. Place asparagus spears over chicken, and cover with the rest of the soup. Sprinkle the crumbs, parsley, almonds, and melted butter over the top. • Bake at 375° for about 20 minutes, uncovered, until topping is brown. May be prepared ahead, covered with foil, and refrigerated. Also good when warmed over.

Brick Beef Stew

Serves 6

bacon fat or cooking oil
1 onion, sliced
2 pounds beef chuck steak,
cut in cubes, or stew beef
1 can tomato soup
2 beef bouillon cubes
2 bay leaves

8 carrots, diced
8 stalks celery, diced
3 to 5 onions, quartered
1 small turnip, chopped
6 whole small potatoes
salt and pepper to taste

• Using a heavy-bottomed saucepan with a tightly fitting cover, sauté the sliced onion until slightly golden in the bacon fat or cooking oil. Add meat, turn heat to high, and quickly sear on all sides. • Turn heat to medium-low and add tomato soup, 3 soup cans of water, bouillon cubes, and bay leaves. Stir well, then add the carrots and celery. • Cover and simmer for 20 minutes and remove bay leaves. Simmer for another 2 hours and 40 minutes.

• Cook the onions, turnips, and potatoes separately and add to stew during the last few minutes for flavor. • This is a recipe with leeway—amounts may vary and results are still good. Tastes even better the next day.

Claire Lee Chennault

1890–1958

In his early days as an Army Air Corps pilot, Claire Chennault led the "Three Men on a Flying Trapeze" aerobatic team; later, the fighter tactics he devised made the American Volunteer Group, the "Flying Tigers," a formidable combat unit in China during World War II. Its outstanding skill and courage gave American morale a much needed boost at the outset of the war, and proved that the Japanese could be beaten in the air. General Chennault was given command of the 14th United States Air Force in China shortly after the United States entered the war. *Recipes from Mrs. Claire L. Chennault*

Oriental Salad Serves 4

6 cucumbers
½ tablespoon curry powder
2 tablespoons sesame oil
2 tablespoons vinegar
½ tablespoon honey
few drops of fresh orange juice
peel of 1 orange, grated
1 tablespoon tartar sauce

Garnish
hard-boiled egg, chopped
raisins
slices of orange or pineapple

• Wash cucumbers in water to which a dash of sugar and salt has been added. • Remove ends of cucumbers and seed. Cut into quarters lengthwise and lightly crush with the back of a heavy knife or other heavy object. • Mix the curry powder, sesame oil, vinegar, honey, orange juice, peel, and tartar sauce. Marinate the cucumbers in this for 1 or 2 hours in the refrigerator. • To serve, sprinkle with hard-boiled egg, raisins, and slices of orange or pineapple. Serve with crabmeat, small shrimp, lobster, or cold sliced chicken.

Concubine Delight

Serves 6-8

2 pounds chicken fillet
(white meat, sliced)
3 egg whites, lightly beaten
dash salt
dash pepper
2 tablespoons Cointreau
1 tablespoon honey
½ pound snow peas (or
green peppers, sliced)
12 dried mushrooms,
soaked at least 6 hours or
overnight, sliced

2 or 3 slices ham or bacon,
minced
2 scallions, sliced
peanut or salad oil
½ fresh ginger kernel,
minced, or 1 tablespoon
chopped preserved
ginger
1 tablespoon cornstarch
¼ cup chicken broth
¼ cup soy sauce
lemon juice to taste

• Mix chicken slices with beaten egg white, salt, pepper, 1 tablespoon Cointreau, and ½ tablespoon honey. • Sauté snow peas or green pepper, mushrooms, ham or bacon, and scallions in oil in a large skillet. • In another skillet, sauté chicken. Add ginger. • In a small saucepan, blend cornstarch with chicken broth, soy sauce, lemon juice, remaining honey, and remaining Cointreau. Bring to boiling, stirring constantly; boil 1 minute or until slightly thickened to make sauce. Remove from heat. • Mix snow pea and chicken mixtures in the larger skillet. Lightly sauté again. Pour in hot sauce.

• Serve with hot rice cooked in tomato juice, or with noodles, or on toast. May be prepared the day before and reheated before serving.

Jacqueline Cochran
19–?–1980

In thirty-five years of flying, ingenuity and persistance have won "Jackie" Cochran more speed, distance, and altitude records than any other pilot. A poverty-stricken foster child with no shoes and often nothing to eat, she grew up to become one of the first women to fly jet aircraft. She was the first woman to fly faster than the speed of sound in an F-86 Sabre jet fighter. In an attempt to expand the role of women in aviation during World War II, she organized and directed the Women's Airforce Service Pilots (WASP) program. Married to developer and financier Floyd Odlum, the versatile Jacqueline Cochran also owned three cosmetic firms and won prizes for her tatting and needlework. *Recipes from Jacqueline Cochran*

Jacqueline Cochran with the Northrop T-38.

Popinosh   Serves 4

2 cups curd cheese put through a sieve, or 2 cups cottage
   cheese strained through cheesecloth
2 large eggs, or 3 small ones
2 tablespoons flour
½ cup coffee cream
salt to taste

• Break eggs into sieved cheese and stir. Add flour. • Fill a
shallow oblong pan with boiling salted water. Drop a teaspoon of the mixture in it. If it tears apart, add another teaspoon of flour to the mixture. • Using a dessert spoon, put
the mixture into the boiling water. Let the dumplings cook
for 5 or 6 minutes. • Place drained dumplings in a buttered
casserole dish. Pour coffee cream over the top. Bake in a
350° oven for 20 to 25 minutes. It may be served as a side
dish, or a main course for a luncheon.

Pecan Pie   Serves 6-8

1 cup light corn syrup
1 cup dark corn syrup
½ cup butter, melted
5 eggs, beaten
¼ cup sugar
1 teaspoon vanilla
1 cup chopped pecans
½ cup pecan halves
8 or 9-inch unbaked pie crust

• Combine syrups, butter, eggs, sugar, vanilla, and
chopped pecans. Place in a mixer and beat at medium
speed for 2 minutes. • Fill pie shell and arrange pecan
halves on the top in a decorative pattern. Bake at 350° for
45 minutes.

*She says of her youth "I
just ran wild—a real
harum-scarum ragamuf-
fin, hunting the woods
and fishing. I caught
crabs and cooked them
and on special occasions
would stoop to 'conquer'
a chicken. . . . I de-
veloped an interesting
technique to catch these
chickens. It consisted of a
piece of corn with a hole
bored through it by
which it was attached to
a long string with myself
at the other end. The
chicken having swal-
lowed the corn would
then be gently drawn
toward me and sure
death. The chicken didn't
belong to me, but the
corn didn't belong to the
chicken either." From*
The Stars at Noon *by
Jacqueline Cochran
(Boston and Toronto:
Little, Brown, and Com-
pany, 1954).*

A. Scott Crossfield

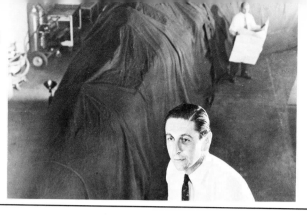

Scott Crossfield in front of
the shrouded X-15 during
its development.

Aeronautical engineer and experimental test pilot, Scott
Crossfield has broken numerous supersonic speed records
in research aircraft such as the Douglas D-558 Skyrocket
and the X-15. He broke a barrier of another sort when
making an emergency landing while testing an F-100 Super
Sabre; the brakes could not stop the plane when it touched
down, and it bored through a hanger. Crossfield recalls:
"Chuck Yeager never let me forget that incident. He drew
many laughs at congregations of pilots by opening his talk,
'Well, the sonic wall was mine. The hangar wall was
Crossfield's.' "* He was the first to fly at twice the speed of
sound, and also was closely involved in the development
of the X-15 as both an engineer and a test pilot. He is now
a technical consultant to the Committee on Science and
Technology of the House of Representatives. *Recipe from
A. Scott Crossfield*

Dry Martini   Serves any number

7 watt light bulb (can be used indefinitely)
1 bottle dry vermouth (can be used indefinitely)
1 bottle gin (per recipe)
1 green unstuffed olive (optional)

• Shine 7-watt bulb through vermouth to impinge and
pass through gin, 1 to 5 minutes to taste. • Turn out light,
drink dry martinis, and will vermouth to heirs.

---

*From *Always Another Dawn: The Story of a Rocket Test Pilot* by
A. Scott Crossfield and Clay Blair, Jr. (Cleveland: World Publishing
Company, 1960).

Betty Skelton Frankman

Although women have at last gained entrance into the astronaut corps, they were excluded at the beginning of the program. However, in 1960 Betty Frankman spent four months discussing the problems of women in space with the National Aeronautics and Space Administration, and experiencing some of the training the astronauts received. The seven astronauts called her "No. 7½." An aerobatic flyer and stunt pilot, she has established several flying records and won the Women's National Aerobatic Championship for four years in a row in the Pitts Special biplane, *Lil' Stinker. Recipes from Betty Skelton Frankman*

Tonga Tabu Grill Serves 8

24 ounces Burgundy wine
1 jar chili sauce
8 ounces honey
3 teaspoons ground ginger
8 ounces teriyaki sauce
8 lemons
3 onions, diced
4 tablespoons cracked pepper
6 to 8-pound eye-of-round beef roast

● Combine wine, chili sauce, honey, ginger, and teriyaki sauce. Squeeze six of the lemons for their juice and add to mixture. ● Place roast in a deep dish and pour sauce over. Slice remaining lemons and place on top. Cover and marinate overnight in refrigerator. ● Place the roast on the grill or on a spit over a charcoal fire. Turn as desired until done, brushing occasionally with the marinade. Cook approximately 1½ hours.

Betty Skelton Frankman and her Pitts Special bi-plane.

Snow Cake   Serves 12

3 envelopes unflavored gelatin
1½ cups water
3 teaspoons lemon juice
1 cup sugar
20-ounce can crushed pineapple
10 ounces nondairy whipped topping
1 large can angel-flake coconut
13-ounce angel food cake, broken into pieces

• Dissolve gelatin in ½ cup cold water. Add 1 cup boiling water, lemon juice, and sugar. Mix well and refrigerate until syrupy. • Add pineapple and its juice to the mixture. Fold in whipped topping, coconut, and the pieces of angel food cake. • Pour into a 3-quart oblong glass pan and cover. Refrigerate overnight before serving.

Royal D. Frey

This was dreamed up by one of my fellow 'Kriegies' in Stalag Luft I, Barth, Germany, during the famine of 1944-45. *About November 1944, the Germans stopped giving us Red Cross parcels and we went strictly on German-supplied rations of sour black bread, frozen rutabagas, and rotten horse meat. This diet was estimated at 700 to 800 calories a day and as we gradually lost weight and our hunger grew, our thoughts turned more and more to food and less and less to liberation and girls. Some character dreamed up the attached recipe and the more we dwelled on it, the more we wanted to throttle him. Anyway, once I got home in June 1945, I whipped it up several times and it was delicious.*

A leading authority of aviation history, especially on the area of World War I aviation, Royal Frey is curator of the United States Air Force Museum at Wright-Patterson Air Force Base in Ohio. A World War II P-38 pilot, he learned his recipe the hard way; he was a prisoner-of-war for fifteen months after bailing out of his burning plane in Germany. *Recipe and comments from Royal D. Frey*

AAF POW's Delight   Serves a variable number

Fig Newtons
chocolate syrup
vanilla ice cream

● Spread a layer of softened ice cream in a rectangular glass dish. ● Top with a layer of Fig Newtons. Pour on a layer of chocolate syrup. Repeat this procedure twice. ● Freeze until hard. To serve, remove from freezer and cut into blocks, and eat with a fork as it gradually becomes warm and softens.

Ernest K. Gann

Ernest Gann prepares to take his reproduction Sopwith F-1 Camel out for a spin.

An adventurer and confirmed vagabond, Ernest Gann has flown or sailed to the far corners of the earth. He began his flying career in his twenties as a stunt flier. After flying for a commercial airline and the Air Transport Command in World War II, he took up writing, incorporating his own experiences into many successful short stories and novels on aviation including *Fate is the Hunter*, his autobiography, and *The High and the Mighty.* He is still an active pilot and author. *Recipe from Ernest K. Gann*

Gann's Cheese Fondue Serves 4

1 clove garlic
1½ pounds Gruyère or Swiss cheese, grated
1 cup dry white wine
4 teaspoons cornstarch
3 tablespoons kirsch
salt to taste
1 loaf French bread, cubed

• Rub a heavy sauce pan with the peeled garlic clove. Add cheese and place over very low heat. As it starts to melt, add the white wine. Stir over low heat until wine and cheese are thoroughly blended. • Dissolve cornstarch in the kirsch and stir this into the cheese mixture. Continue cooking and stirring until the mixture is thickened and creamy. Season to taste with salt. • Keep hot over an alcohol flame or in an electric fondue pot. Serve with cubes of French bread to be speared with long-handled forks and then dipped into the hot fondue. If the cheese mixture gets too thick, add more kirsch.

George H. Gay

The only pilot who came back from the Torpedo Squadron 8 attack on the Japanese carriers in the Battle of Midway during World War II was George Gay. Then a young ensign, Gay tells his heroic story in a recent book, *Sole Survivor*, published thirty-seven years after his experience. On June 4, 1942, fifteen Douglas TBDs of Gay's squadron took off from the carrier *Hornet* in an attempt to locate the Japanese fleet approaching Midway Island. The squadron located the enemy and attacked at once without any protective cover. Ensign Gay, his plane shot down, found himself swimming about in the middle of the Japanese navy, when incredibly two objects from his plane rose to the surface—his seat cushion and life raft. He was alone at sea concealing himself from enemy pilots for about thirty hours before an American patrol plane spotted him and made a daring rescue. Captain Gay, who was given the Navy Cross, remained in the navy until after World War II. This was followed by thirty years as a pilot for Trans World Airlines. *Recipe and comments from George H. Gay*

Born in Waco, Texas, we were far from affluent, so I began early to be thrifty and have always disliked seeing food wasted. In 1945, my pay as a new TWA copilot was $180 a month, but I still had the guts to ask a gal to marry me, because I thought I might have some kind of future. We did not exactly starve, but we did have to devise ways to avoid it. Ground beef was inexpensive at the time, but we wanted some way to spice it up. As time went on and our financial situation improved, we began to expand on the original recipe for my favorite dish. It is called "Tessie's Goulash" after my wife. Whenever you find yourself wondering what to prepare for a hungry bunch, just grind up a batch; I will guarantee it to be a crowd pleaser.

Tessie's Goulash

Serves 4

1 small package elbow
  macaroni
1 pound ground beef
cooking oil
1 clove garlic, minced
1 green pepper, chopped
1 16-ounce can of tomatoes
1 8-ounce can tomato sauce
1 6-ounce can mushrooms

parsley flakes, in
  moderation
1 onion, chopped
Cheddar cheese chunks, to
  taste
1 6-ounce can ripe pitted
  olives, each cut in half
salt and pepper
1 package American cheese,
  sliced

• Cook macaroni, drain, and reserve • Brown beef in cooking oil, drain grease. • Add garlic and green peppers and cook for 5 minutes. Add tomatoes, tomato sauce, mushrooms, parsley, onion, Cheddar cheese, and olives. • Mix with cooked macaroni; salt and pepper to taste. • Transfer to a casserole and cover with sliced American cheese. • Bake in 350° oven for 1 hour. *Serve with tossed green salad and garlic bread.*

Barry M. Goldwater

Although Barry Goldwater was unable to become a fighter pilot because of poor eyesight, he did become a Service Pilot in World War II. Ironically, he ended up leading the unprecedented flight of P-47 Thunderbolts across the North Atlantic for delivery to Europe in 1943. In 1948 Goldwater organized the Arizona Air National Guard, and served as its chief of staff until he was elected senator in 1952. Knowing of his interest in aviation, manufacturers have invited him to fly practically every new airplane built. A strong political supporter of flight, he was a major force behind the construction of the National Air and Space Museum. *Recipe and comments from Barry M. Goldwater*

There is nothing I like better than just plain Navajo Fry Bread, which is unleavened, well-kneaded, with the air beaten out of it, and then fried in deep fat.

Navajo Fry Bread
3 cups white flour
3 tablespoons baking powder
3 tablespoons salt
warm water
lard

• Mix flour, baking powder, and salt. Add warm water, a little at a time, to make a soft but not sticky dough. Knead well. • Tear off about one to two tablespoons of the dough and stretch and pat until thin. Drop into deep, sizzling hot lard. Brown on both sides. Repeat with rest of dough. Drain on paper towels. • Serve at once.

Clifford W. Henderson

Clifford Henderson flying in his official scout plane of the National Air Races.

Although his first attempt at showmanship at age nine netted a gate of one dollar, Clifford Henderson grew up to become the P. T. Barnum of aviation. Various national racing events had been conducted since 1920 under the aegis of the National Aeronautics Association, but it was Henderson, in 1928, who persuaded them to go "pro," thus attracting such sponsors as Bendix and Thompson, and making the meets important in the development of aviation. He said of the air races, "Speed without efficiency or weight-carrying ability is no accomplishment. Nor is high payload a definite advance if the ship is able to cruise only a few miles faster than railroad trains. The $100,000 prize money offered by the Air Race Corporation and the designation of requirements for the numerous events furnish a stimulus to aircraft builders to combine these important factors."* *Recipe from Clifford W. Henderson*

Henderson's Hot Buttered Rum   Serves 1
2 jiggers light rum
4 heaping teaspoons brown sugar
hot water
pinch of ground cloves
pinch of ground nutmeg
2 teaspoons butter

• Pour rum in a heat-proof glass. Add the brown sugar and mix. • Fill glass with boiling water and add cloves and nutmeg. • Add butter and stir until melted.

*From "Mystery Planes to Speed at Air Races" by Clifford Henderson, *The Chicago Visitor,* August 1930.

Beverly Howard
1914–1971

Beverly Howard performs his most famous stunt—cutting a ribbon held between two poles, while flying upside down.

"Bevo" Howard helped to pay for his flying lessons at the age of sixteen by making parachute jumps and selling airplane rides. By the time he was twenty-one, he was president of an airline. His interest in aerobatics led him to acquire a Buecker–Jungmeister, brought over from Germany on the *Hindenburg*. With this plane he developed many innovative stunts, including cutting a ribbon stretched between two poles while flying upside down. A familiar figure in air shows in the United States, Howard also won many international aerobatic championships and was called "the ambassador of the air." *Recipe from Mrs. Beverly Howard*

Upside-down Cake

¼ pound butter, melted
3¾ pounds brown sugar
½ cup pecans (optional)
1 to 1½ pounds fresh or
    canned sliced pineapple
    or peaches

Batter
1 cup butter
1 cup sugar
2 large or 3 medium eggs
2 cups flour
2 teaspoons baking powder
½ cup milk
vanilla

• Place the melted butter and brown sugar in a heavy iron skillet or cake pan. Mix together and spread evenly over the bottom of the pan. Sprinkle with pecan nutmeats if desired. • Arrange the fruit slices closely on sugar. Set aside. • Cream butter and add sugar gradually. Beat in the eggs, one at a time, until smooth. • Sift together flour and baking powder; add to batter alternately with milk. Stir in vanilla to taste. • Pour mixture over fruit and bake at 350° for about 45 minutes, or until a toothpick inserted in the center of the cake comes out clean. Remove from oven and immediately turn upside down on a plate.

This recipe is from an old family cookbook.

Benjamin S. Kelsey

This noted engineer and test pilot learned to fly at the age of fourteen and owned and operated a Jenny until the state of Connecticut made him desist because he was under twenty-one. That was soon solved; he had the law changed. In over half a century of flying, General Kelsey's career has spanned a great amount of aviation history—from the early fragile crafts to the latest supersonic aircraft. In his early days in the Army Air Corps, he became associated with Jimmy Doolittle and in 1929 participated with him in the world's first blind flight, using instruments only. After distinguished service in the European Theater during World War II, he returned to the United States and various top assignments at Wright-Patterson Air Force Base, Air Force Headquarters in Washington, D.C., and a stint on the faculty of the War College. He retired in 1955 as a brigadier general. Later, he was Hunsacker Professor of Aeronautics at Massachusetts Institute of Technology where many years before he had received his Master of Science degree in aeronautical engineering. In 1980, General Kelsey became the second occupant of the Charles A. Lindbergh Chair at the National Air and Space Museum where he is researching military aviation from 1927 to 1940. *Recipes from Benjamin S. Kelsey*

Benjamin's Brownies   Makes 16 to 20 bars
1 cup flour
2 cups sugar
4 eggs
½ pound butter or margarine
4 squares unsweetened chocolate
pinch of salt

• Stir together flour and sugar. Mix in eggs, one at a time, and beat thoroughly. • Melt butter or margarine over low heat. Break chocolate into pieces and stir into butter, just until melted. Add salt. • Beat together the two mixtures until well blended. Turn into a well-greased 9 × 12-inch pan, and bake at 350° for about 20 minutes or until edges begin to pull away from sides. Do not overcook. • Cool and cut into bars.

Steak Teriyaki Serves 4

1 large flank steak
prepared mustard
teriyaki sauce
¼ cup water
½ cup butter
1 pound mushrooms, sliced

• Pierce the steak with a fork and spread both sides liber-
ally with mustard. Place in a 9 × 11-inch baking pan. Add
enough teriyaki sauce to coat the steak well and cover the
bottom of the pan. Marinate for at least 1 hour. • Add
water to pan. Place under broiler and cook 7 minutes on
each side. • Melt butter in a large skillet. Cook mushrooms over medium heat until soft and reduced in volume.
Scrape coagulated juices from steak pan and stir in with
mushrooms. • Slice steak very thinly, across the grain of
the meat, and serve smothered with mushrooms.

Henry T. Merrill

Rushing sick babies to hospitals, ferrying sacks of mail through the night, flying presidents hither and yon, "Dick" Merrill has logged 44,111 hours flying time, much of it as an Eastern Airlines flight captain. He began his career as a barnstormer in the 1920s and continued in the same adventurous spirit. In 1937 he won the Harmon trophy by flying photographs of the *Hindenburg* disaster to England and returning with pictures of King George's coronation, setting six new records in the process. He is now curator of the Shannon Air Museum in Fredricksburg, Virginia, which houses such planes as Spads, and the Mailwings of his early days. *Recipes from Henry T. Merrill*

Airmail Meatloaf

Serves 4-6

½ cup chopped onion
½ cup celery
¼ cup butter
1 small green pepper, chopped
1 teaspoon salt
½ teaspoon white pepper

2 eggs, slightly beaten
1 cup bread crumbs
1 cup consommé
1½ pounds ground beef
½ cup tomato juice

• Brown the onion and celery in 2 tablespoons of the butter. Remove from heat and add the green pepper, salt, pepper, eggs, and bread crumbs. • Mix this with ½ cup consommé and add to meat. Add balance of consommé and work into meat until it is absorbed. • Fill a greased loaf pan with the mixture. Bake at 350° for 30 minutes. • Mix tomato juice and remaining butter, melted. Pour half of this over the meat and cook 15 minutes, then add the other half of the sauce and cook 15 minutes more. Brown top under broiler if you wish.

Eggs à la Merrill   Serves 8

4 trout fillets, each cut in half
1¼ cups milk
1½ cups flour
½ teaspoon salt
½ teaspoon white pepper
cooking oil
16 large eggs

• Soak fillets in milk for 5 minutes, then roll in flour, salt, and pepper to coat evenly. Deep or shallow fry in hot oil, 375°, until crisp and brown, about 5 minutes. Remove from oil and drain on paper towels. • Poach the eggs. • Place a piece of trout on a heated plate, top with two poached eggs, then cover evenly with Hollandaise sauce.

Hollandaise Sauce
8 large egg yolks, lightly beaten
4 tablespoons lemon juice
2 pounds melted butter
1 teaspoon salt
¼ teaspoon cayenne pepper

• Stir together egg yolks, lemon juice, salt, and cayenne in a heavy saucepan over very low heat, or in a double boiler over barely simmering water. • Stirring constantly with a wire wisk, add butter slowly, a tablespoon at a time. It is important to add the butter this way so that it will be absorbed by the egg yolks and will not curdle. Stir until well mixed and serve at once.

Jerrie Mock

A lifetime interest in flying led this Columbus, Ohio, housewife on a solo round-the-world flight. Following in the footsteps of Amelia Earhart, Jerrie Mock became the first woman to pilot an aircraft around the world and to fly across both the Atlantic and Pacific oceans in 1964. In 1965 she also set a new speed record on a flight from Columbus to Las Vegas. She is interested in international cuisine, especially central European, African, and Asian specialities. *Recipes and comments from Jerrie Mock*

Bastilia is usually served as a first course in a traditional meal of couscous in many parts of North Africa and the Middle East. I first experienced these dishes in Morocco in the spring of 1964 when I landed there after completing a flight from the Azores. I was in the early stages of the first woman-around-the-world flight in the Cessna 180. I would appreciate your attributing these recipes to 'Jerrie' Mock, rather then 'Geraldine,' as I suspect that all 'Geraldines' get air sick!

Bastilia

Serves 8-10

2½ to 3 pounds chicken legs and breasts, or four fat pigeons
1¼ cups plus 1 tablespoon butter
1 cup chopped onions
½ teaspoon coriander
1 teaspoon harissa*
½ teaspoon cumin
½ teaspoon dried mint
1 tablespoon finely chopped parsley
1 teaspoon ground ginger
¼ teaspoon saffron

½ teaspoon salt
4 teaspoons cinnamon
1 cup water
6 eggs
1½ cups blanched chopped almonds
3 tablespoons sugar
1 package phyllo (strudel leaves), found in mideastern food stores
3 tablespoons vegetable oil
3 tablespoons powdered sugar

*Harissa may be found in an Arabic grocery store, or substitute the following:

1 6-ounce can tomato paste
2 tablespoons cayenne pepper
¼ teaspoon salt
¼ teaspoon coriander
¼ teaspoon cumin powder
¼ cup olive oil

• Combine all ingredients well. To store, film with olive oil, cover tightly, and refrigerate.

Jerrie Mock descends from the cockpit of the Cessna 180 Spirit of Columbus *after her round-the-world flight.*

• Brown chicken or pigeons in 6 tablespoons of the butter. Remove to a plate. Add onions to pan and cook until translucent. Add coriander, harissa, cumin, mint, parsley, ginger, saffron, salt, and ½ teaspoon cinnamon. Mix in water and bring to a boil. Return chicken to pan, cover, and cook over low heat until tender. Drain chicken and reserve broth. Cut meat into pieces about 2 inches by 1 inch, discarding bones and skin. • Bring reserved broth to a boil. Beat eggs lightly and add, stirring until softly scrambled and most of broth is absorbed. Remove from heat.

• Brown chopped almonds in 4 tablespoons of the butter. Drain and mix with sugar and ½ teaspoon cinnamon.

• Spread 6 sheets of phyllo so they overlap in a circle, pinwheel fashion. Fold 2 sheets in half and place in center for reinforcement. • Spread almond mixture in an 8-inch circle in the center of phyllo leaves. Cover this with ½ of the egg mixture. Put pieces of chicken in a neat layer on top of this and cover with the rest of the eggs. • Fold up center pieces of phyllo to encircle all layers of stuffing. Melt 8 tablespoons of butter and brush on exposed phyllo (open leaves) and fold each sheet up over the stuffing separately. Brush each sheet as you proceed. Before the last sheet of folded phyllo is pulled up, add 2 more folded sheets to the top of the stack to make the crust firmer.

• Melt 3 tablespoons butter with 3 tablespoons vegetable oil in a large, heavy skillet. Slide bastilia into skillet and brown over moderate heat. When golden, slide onto plate, place another plate over the top. Hold firmly and invert the plates and bastilia. Slide bastilia back into skillet and brown on other side. • Sprinkle with powdered sugar and 3 teaspoons cinnamon. Cut in wedges to serve.

Couscous

Serves 6

¾ cup dry chick peas
  (garbanzos)
2 tablespoons margarine
1½ pounds lean boneless
  lamb, beef, or camel meat,
  cubed
1½ cups coarsely chopped
  onion
2 garlic cloves, minced
1 teaspoon salt
1 teaspoon pepper
1-inch of stick cinnamon
¼ teaspoon allspice
½ teaspoon dried mint

1 teaspoon oregano
1 teaspoon cumin powder
1 teaspoon coriander
1 teaspoon harissa*
2 cups canned or fresh
  tomatoes
2 large carrots, cut in chunks
1 large potato, quartered
1 cup zuchini squash, cubed
4 tablespoons melted butter
17 ounces of couscous
  (found in a mideastern
  food store)

• Put chick peas in a pan with two cups of water. Bring to a boil, and cook for 2 minutes. Remove from heat and let chick peas soak for 1 hour (or soak overnight), until ready to be added to the meat. • Brown meat in margarine in the bottom of a *couscousier* or a large steamer. Add onion and cook about 10 minutes. Add spices with just enough water to keep food from burning and braise meat on low heat. Check every 15 minutes and add small amounts of water when needed. • When almost tender, add vegetables, chick peas, and more water. Simmer for another ½ hour. (Other vegetables may be used, such as green beans, turnips, pumpkin, squash, cabbage, or peas.) • Fifteen minutes after adding vegetables, put dry couscous in a bowl and cover with water to soak (it will swell in size). Soak 15 minutes; then put it in the top part of a steamer and place over the steaming meat and vegetables. If steam escapes, put a damp cloth in the space between the top and bottom of the steamer. Steam for ½ hour. • The couscous will be hot and moist with the flavoring of the broth, vegetables, and meat. Pour melted butter over couscous.

It can be served in three bowls: one for broth, one for couscous, one for the meat and vegetables. However, according to Bedouin custom, the couscous, meat, and vegetables are traditionally served from a single central bowl. The diners, seated around it, dip in and roll the mixture into a ball using, traditionally, only the right hand.

*See recipe for Bastilia.

Jeanette Piccard

Jeanette Piccard gives reporters an interview at the conclusion of her 1934 flight 10 miles into the stratosphere with her husband Dr. Jean Piccard.

The first woman to explore the earth's upper atmosphere in 1934, Jeanette Piccard holds the women's record for a free balloon ascent of 57,559 feet. Her late husband Jean Piccard was a famed aerospace scientist who conducted numerous stratospheric tests. She worked for the women's right to vote, won in 1920, and now says, "We figured we had it made and sat back on our fannies."* Of her flight experiences, she "never felt discriminated against, in the air at least—you see, I was the token, the only one, hence no threat."* An aeronaut of many talents, she holds degrees in philosophy, education, psychology, and organic chemistry, and has been a consultant to the National Aeronautics and Space Administration and the Office of Naval Research. She was recently ordained as a priest of the Episcopal Church. *Recipes and comments from Jeanette Piccard*

Kidney and Mushrooms   Serves 3-6

This can be served immediately, when the rice and a salad are ready, or left to simmer for several hours while you go fishing, hunting, or flying. It is excellent for a hunt breakfast or a balloon brunch. The rice can cook while you serve the morning juice.

1 veal or baby beef kidney (the veal is better, but hard to find)	2 tablespoons all-purpose flour
	½ cup water
	½ teaspoon salt
1 tablespoon cooking oil	1 to 2 teaspoons marjoram
½ to 1 pound mushrooms	1 to 2 teaspoons curry powder

• With a sharp knife cut the meat from the fat core in bite-size pieces to get rid of the fat and strings. This does not have to be done too carefully. The more meat you get the less waste, but don't wear yourself out. • Place oil in a heavy-bottomed saucepan. Heat and brown kidney pieces lightly on all sides. Do not cook too long, as overcooking at this point makes the kidney tough. Remove to a plate or bowl. • Sauté the mushrooms in the cooking oil. Add flour and stir well. Add water, stirring rapidly to make a smooth gravy. Add the kidney and its juices, salt, and herbs. Lower heat to simmer—never overheat the kidney. May be kept on low heat up to 1 hour. Serve over rice.

*From "Getting Women's Year Off to a Flying Start" by Emily Fisher, The Washington Post, January 13, 1975.

Elwood Quesada

Involved in aviation throughout his long career, Elwood Quesada was a relief pilot in the week-long 1929 flight of the *Question Mark,* which demonstrated the techniques of midair refueling. During World War II he was in charge of the 12th Fighter Command in Africa, was deputy commander of the Northwest African Air Force, and later took over the 9th Tactical Air Command during the invasion of Normandy. At the close of the war, Quesada became assistant chief of staff of the United States Air Force. He organized and was the first to head the Tactical Air Command. He retired from the military in 1951 to enter private industry and government. His many activities included serving as vice president and director of Lockheed Aircraft, and as the first administrator of the Federal Aviation Agency. *Recipe from Elwood Quesada*

Coffee Ice Cream Supreme   Serves 8

2 quarts coffee ice cream
1 quart vanilla ice cream
12 macaroons, crushed
2 squares unsweetened chocolate, shaved; or powdered
  cocoa

• Line a three-quart mold with the coffee ice cream. Fill center with vanilla ice cream and pack down well. • Press half of the macaroon crumbs into the ice cream. Cover with waxed paper and freeze for several hours. • Remove from freezer 15 minutes before serving and unmold on a platter. Garnish with remaining macaroons, and sprinkle with shaved chocolate or cocoa. Serve with Hot Fudge Sauce.

Hot Fudge Sauce

2 squares unsweetened   ½ cup milk
  chocolate   3 tablespoons butter
1 cup sugar   1 tablespoon brandy (optional)

• Break chocolate into bits and place in a saucepan. Add sugar and milk and cook over low heat, stirring constantly, until chocolate is melted and mixture thickens slightly.
• Remove from heat and add butter and brandy. Stir until butter is melted.

Cliff Robertson

Interested in flying since his youth, Cliff Robertson began collecting planes in the early 1960s. He has flown several from his collection for films and television, including "A Place of Dreams," a television special about the history of aviation as presented in the National Air and Space Museum. His diversified interests include collecting antique aircraft, and acting, writing, and directing. *Recipe from Cliff Robertson*

Spaghetti Vongole   Serves 4-6

1 box vermicelli spaghetti
5 tablespoons olive oil
1 cup finely chopped scallions
½ cup finely chopped celery
5 tablespoons Chablis wine
fresh ground pepper to taste
½ teaspoon paprika
4 cloves garlic, minced
2 cups finely chopped canned clams

• Cook spaghetti according to package directions. • While this is cooking, heat olive oil in a skillet and sauté scallions and celery slowly over a low flame for about 10 minutes. Stir in wine, pepper, paprika, and garlic. • Add clams and cook for another three minutes. • Drain spaghetti and toss with clam mixture. Serve at once.

Neta Snook Southern

Neta Snook Southern poses with Amelia Earhart in front of the training plane.

An early aviation pioneer, Neta Southern took her first flying lessons in 1917. In 1918 she was hired by the British Air Ministry as their representative in Canada and the United States to expedite deliveries of planes, parts, and engines for the war effort. In the spring of 1920 she made her first solo flight and earned her living as a barnstormer, flying a plane she had rebuilt herself, and also gave flying lessons—all unusual activities for a woman in that era. In December 1920 an attractive young woman came to her to learn to fly—Amelia Earhart. Thus began Amelia Earhart's flying career. *Recipe from Neta Snook Southern*

Bread and Butter Pickles   Makes 2-3 pints

1 quart sliced cucumbers
1 sliced onion
1 green pepper, cut in rings
1 cup sugar
1 tablespoon mustard seed
½ cup vinegar
½ cup water
1 teaspoon celery seed

• Combine cucumbers with onion and green pepper in a bowl. Cover with salted water and let stand for 3 hours. Drain well. • Mix the sugar, mustard seed, vinegar, water, and celery seed. Add to the vegetables and bring to a boil. • Seal in sterilized jars while hot.

Carl Andrew Spaatz

1891–1974

As a member of the 1st Aero Squadron of the United States Army, "Tooey" Spaatz was one of the first twenty-five Americans to earn wings in 1916. Although his combat flying in World War I was limited to only a few weeks, he shot down three Fokkers. Between the wars, General Spaatz commanded the *Question Mark,* which established a 150-hour endurance record in 1929 using midair refueling, an important first step in the development of long-range aircraft. One of the great air leaders in World War II, he became the first chief of staff of the United States Air Force in 1947. *Recipe from Mrs. Carl A. Spaatz*

White Gazpacho   Serves 4

2 cucumbers
1 small onion
1 garlic clove
1 pint sour cream
¾ cup plain yogurt
1 cup chicken stock
Tabasco sauce
salt and pepper

Garnish
chopped tomatoes
chives

• Peel and seed the cucumbers, and chop finely. Mince onion. Crush garlic with the blade of a knife or put through a garlic press. • Mix cucumbers, onion, and garlic with the sour cream, yogurt, and chicken stock. Season to taste. • Chill overnight. Serve icy cold, garnished with chopped tomatoes and chives.

Louise M. Thaden
1905–1979

Since I can remember, from the time when I was seven and jumped off the barn under an oversized umbrella, I've wanted to fly. For years it was merely a passive ambition. It was like the moon–completely unattainable. *

Louise Thaden nevertheless learned to fly. She won the first Women's Air Derby in 1929 and was the first woman to win the Bendix Transcontinental Air Race in 1936. She also held many speed and altitude records in general aviation. Until her death, she was the owner of the Thaden Engineering Company. *Recipe from Louise M. Thaden*

*High, Wide, and Frightened by Louise M. Thaden (New York: Stackpole and Sons, 1938)

Louise Thaden in 1929.

Quiche Lorraine   Makes 1 pie

9-inch unbaked pie shell
4 strips bacon
1 onion, thinly sliced
1 cup Swiss cheese
¼ cup Parmesan cheese, grated
4 eggs, slightly beaten
2 cups heavy cream
¼ teaspoon nutmeg
½ teaspoon salt
¼ teaspoon white pepper

● Preheat over to 450°. ● Weight the center of the pie shell with dry beans or rice wrapped in foil, or prick slightly with a fork. Bake 5 to 10 minutes, until pastry is set but not brown. ● Cook bacon until crisp and remove from skillet. Sauté onion in bacon fat until transparent. ● Crumble bacon and sprinkle with the onion and cheeses over the partially baked crust. ● Combine eggs, cream, nutmeg, salt, and pepper and pour over onion and cheese mixture. ● Bake 15 minutes at 450°; then reduce oven temperature to 350° and bake for another 25 minutes or until a toothpick inserted 1 inch from pastry edge comes out clean.

Makes 10-12 servings as an appetizer or 4-6 servings as a main course.

Roscoe Turner

1895–1971

Roscoe Turner and Gilmore.

A flamboyant showman, Roscoe Turner favored powder-blue military-type uniforms of his own design and flew with his companion Gilmore, a lion cub, promoting the products of an oil company. Registering as Roscoe and Gilmore, they often shared rooms on the road until the growing lion became too big for the cockpit. As a racing pilot, Turner received numerous trophies and established many speed records in planes which he helped to design and build. He was the only three-time winner of the Charles E. Thompson Trophy which is awarded when a new world's high-speed record is established. *Recipe and comments from Mrs. Madonna M. Wells, the former Mrs. Roscoe Turner*

Roscoe Turner's Sweet Potato Pie   Serves 6-8

For those who have not heard of sweet potato pie, this is quite good. Since my husband was from Mississippi, he felt it a necessity to have sweet potato pie on occasion so this is a northerner's answer (mine) to the request.

4 tablespoons butter
½ cup sugar
3 eggs, separated
1 teaspoon vanilla
½ teaspoon nutmeg
½ teaspoon cinnamon
2 cups sweet potatoes, cooked and mashed
1 cup rich milk or half-and-half
9-inch unbaked pie shell

• Cream butter and sugar. Add beaten egg yolks, vanilla, nutmeg, cinnamon, potatoes, milk; mix well. • Beat egg whites until stiff and fold into potato mixture. • Pour into pie shell and bake at 425° for 15 minutes; then lower heat to 350° and bake for 40 minutes longer.

Fay Gillis Wells

Fay Wells.

Fay Wells became the first woman pilot to join the Caterpiller Club, in 1929. Membership required a parachute jump from a disabled aircraft to save your life—as Fay Wells said, "Although membership was optional I thought it was highly desirable!" At this time she also became the first airplane saleswoman for Curtiss Flying Service. In Russia during the early 1930s as a correspondent for Associated Press and the *New York Herald Tribune,* she assisted Wiley Post with the logistics of his record breaking solo around-the-world flight. Along with Amelia Earhart, she was an organizer and charter member of the 99 Club of licensed women pilots. Her varied career has ranged from buying strategic war material in Portuguese West Africa during World War II to White House correspondent. *Comments from Fay Gillis Wells*

Sweet and Sour Stuffed Cabbage Rolls   Serves 4

This recipe was created for Fay Gillis Wells by David Young of Paul Young's Restaurant in Washington, D.C., for the American Newspaper Women's Club's gourmet gala in December 1979.

1 large head cabbage
3 onions
30 ounces canned tomatoes, mashed
2 cups plus 2 tablespoons cold water
2 tablespoons brown sugar
juice of 1 lemon
1 teaspoon white vinegar
½ cup raisins
1½ pounds ground beef
1 egg
1 cup cooked rice
2 cloves garlic, finely minced
salt and pepper

• Blanch cabbage in boiling water for about 5 minutes, or until leaves are soft and pliable but not overcooked. Peel off 12 of the outer leaves and reserve. • Chop the remaining cabbage and 2 onions coarsely. Mix in a large saucepan or kettle with tomatoes, 2 cups water, brown sugar, lemon juice, vinegar, raisins, and salt and pepper to taste. Cover and simmer for approximately 15 minutes.
• Prepare filling by mixing beef, egg, rice, garlic, 2 tablespoons water, and remaining onion, grated. Divide this mixture and place on each of the reserved leaves. Roll gently, tucking in the sides of the leaf like an egg roll. • Place, seam side down, into the sauce. Cover and simmer until cooked, about 30 minutes. Adjust seasoning to taste.

Robert M. White

In 1962, Robert White became the fifth person to win astronaut "wings" as pilot of the X-15. This was the first time they had been awarded for a flight in a winged aircraft rather than a spacecraft. Flying six times faster than the speed of sound, he attained an altitude of more than 59 miles above the earth. White has served as commander of the Air Force Flight Test Center at Edwards Air Force Base in California, and is now chief of staff of the 4th Allied Tactical Air Force at Ramstein Air Base in Germany. *Recipe from Robert M. White*

Party Paté   Serves approximately 10

2 cans liver paté
4½ ounces deviled ham (canned)
6 ounces cream cheese
Worcestershire sauce to taste
1 envelope gelatin
½ cup cold water
1 cup beef consommé
¼ cup sherry
crackers

• Mix together the liver paté, deviled ham, cream cheese, and Worcestershire sauce. Set aside. • Dissolve gelatin in cold water. Heat beef consommé with sherry and add softened gelatin; stir until gelatin is dissolved. Pour into the bottom of a lightly greased 1½-quart mold and let it set.

• Spread paté mixture on top. Refrigerate. • Unmold just before serving, and surround with crackers. It is better if made a day ahead.

Alford J. Williams, Jr.
1896–1958

A pioneer of high-speed flying, Al Williams started out as a pitcher for the New York Giants. With the outbreak of World War I, he enlisted as a naval aviator and became interested in aerobatics and racing. In 1923 he won the Pulitzer Trophy for high-speed flying in competition and, while still in the navy, he was awarded the Distinguished Flying Cross for his test-flying achievements. As one of the first proponents of United States air power, he felt that he could better advance this cause as a civilian. As a result, he joined Gulf Oil Corporation in 1933 as manager of the aviation division and flew his plane, the *Gulfhawk,* at air shows all over the world demonstrating precision aerobatics. During World War II, he served as a technical consultant to the Army Air Forces, lecturing and demonstrating fighter techniques. He remained with Gulf until 1951, during which time he also wrote a syndicated column on aviation. *Recipes from Mrs. Alford Williams*

Orange-glazed Pork Chops   Serves 4

4 loin pork chops, 1 inch thick
salt, pepper, and paprika
2 tablespoons water
5 tablespoons sugar
1½ teaspoons cornstarch
¼ teaspoon salt
¼ teaspoon cinnamon
10 whole cloves
2 teaspoons grated orange rind
½ cup orange juice
4 orange slices

• Trim fat from chops, and season with salt, pepper, and paprika. Brown well on both sides in lightly greased skillet. Add water, cover, and cook slowly for 45 minutes or until chops can be cut with a fork. • While chops are cooking, mix together sugar, cornstarch, salt, cinnamon, cloves, orange juice, and rind. Cook over medium heat, stirring constantly, until sauce thickens and becomes transparent. • Top each chop with an orange slice, pour on orange glaze, and let stand for several minutes before serving.

Al Williams.

Green Pea and Bean Salad Serves 4

1 can small green peas
1 can French-style beans
1 small jar pimientos
2 stalks celery, chopped
1 small onion, sliced thin
⅔ cup vinegar
⅔ cup oil
⅔ cup sugar

• Mix all ingredients together in order listed. Cover and refrigerate overnight.

Pumpkin Bread   Makes 1 loaf

8 ounces canned crushed
  pineapple
1 beaten egg
1 cup canned pumpkin
¼ cup melted butter
2¾ cups flour
1 cup sugar
2 teaspoons baking soda
1½ teaspoons pumpkin
  spice
¼ teaspoon salt
½ cup chopped walnuts

• Combine pineapple and juice, egg, pumpkin, and butter. • Sift flour with sugar, baking soda, spice, and salt in bowl. Add pineapple mixture, stir until flour is moist. Add nuts. • Place in a greased and floured loaf pan. Bake at 350° degrees for 1 hour and 10 minutes, or until loaf tests done. Let stand for 10 minutes out of the oven; remove from pan and place on rack to cool.

Steve Wittman

Steve Wittman has been designing and piloting racing aircraft for more than fifty years; his racer "Buster"—now in the National Air and Space Museum's collection—has the second-best overall winning record in air racing. Beginning as a barnstormer in the days when flyers simply landed in any handy unplowed field, Wittman went on to become the first manager of the Oshkosh Airport in Wisconsin which was later renamed Wittman Field. Operator of a flying school and also a test pilot during his long and varied career, he won many events in the National Air Races. *Recipes from Mrs. Steve Wittman*

Steve Wittman rolls out his racer Bonzo.

*From "The Old Man of the Sky" by Miles McNamara, *The Milwaukee Journal,* April 4, 1976

Green Bean Baked Dish

Serves 6-8

3 15-ounce cans whole
  green beans
2 4-ounce cans button
  mushrooms
½ pound bacon
½ cup diced onions
4 tablespoons of bacon fat

3 tablespoons flour
1 cup vegetable juice from
  beans
¾ cup sugar
1 cup tarragon vinegar
salt and pepper to taste

• Drain beans and mushrooms well, saving 1 cup of the bean juice. Mix beans and mushrooms in an 8 × 18-inch baking dish, and set aside. • Fry bacon until crisp and drain on paper towels. Fry onions in bacon fat until wilted, remove from pan, and set aside. • Leave 4 tablespoons of bacon fat in the pan and add flour. Stir until light brown. Add the bean juice, sugar, vinegar, and salt and pepper. Mixture should be thick like gravy. Add the bacon and onions, mix well, and pour over beans and mushrooms.

• Best if covered and refrigerated overnight during which the flavors mingle. Bake at 350° for 45 minutes or until bubbly.

Sugar Cookies

Makes approximately 4 dozen

1 cup white sugar
1 cup powdered sugar
1 cup margarine
1 cup vegetable oil
2 eggs

1 teaspoon vanilla
4½ cups flour
1 teaspoon cream of tartar
½ teaspoon soda
½ teaspoon salt

• Cream together the sugars, margarine, and oil. Beat in the eggs and vanilla. • Mix together the flour, cream of tarter, soda, and salt. Add the margarine mixture. • Roll batter in small balls, about the size of a walnut, and roll in sugar. Place on cookie sheet, and press down with the bottom of a small glass. • Bake at 350° for 15 minutes.

ASTRONAUTS

Michael Collins
Lamb Curry

Charles M. Duke, Jr.
Lunar Bread

Donn F. Eisele
Mongolian Hot Pot

Richard F. Gordon, Jr.
Crêpes with Orange Sauce
Gazpacho

James B. Irwin
Cream of Celery Soup

James A. Lovell, Jr.
Baked Tomatoes Rockefeller
Dill Dip

Edgar D. Mitchell
Country Spare Ribs

Harrison H. Schmitt
Schmitt's Special Chili

Donald K. Slayton
Chili

Thomas P. Stafford
Rice with Green Chilies and Sour Cream
German Cream Cheese Brownies
Chocolate Cheese Cake

John L. Swigert, Jr.
Jacksonville Crisps
Sweet and Sour Barbecued Ribs

Michael Collins

Michael Collins prepares for Gemini 10.

Although he experienced his first taste of flying at the age of ten as a passenger in a Grumman "Widgeon" amphibian, Michael Collins was more excited by tales of his father's first plane ride in a 1911 Wright military plane. Later, as a test pilot at Edwards Air Force Base in California, Collins became interested in space flight. He was the third American to "walk" in space during the Gemini 10 flight, and his career as an astronaut culminated in 1969 when he served as Apollo 11 command-module pilot on the first moon-landing mission. He has been described as the most solitary of human beings during that flight, orbiting the moon alone in the command ship *Columbia,* while Neil Armstrong and Edwin (Buzz) Aldrin explored the lunar surface. Collins accepted an appointment as assistant secretary of state for public affairs in 1970, and in 1971 became director of the National Air and Space Museum. In 1978 he was appointed Under Secretary of the Smithsonian Institution and now serves as vice president of field operations of the Vought Corporation. *Recipe from Michael Collins*

Lamb Curry

Serves 6-10

1 large onion, chopped
4 tablespoons oil
2 tablespoons mild curry powder
2 tablespoons flour
2 bouillon cubes
2 cups boiling water

1 tablespoon paprika
¼ cup dried parsley, or fresh parsley, chopped
dash of Worcestershire sauce
2 tablespoons catsup
3 cups rare cooked lamb, cubed

• Brown onion in oil in a large frying pan and remove from pan. • Add curry powder to remaining oil and stir. Sprinkle in flour and mix with oil over low heat to make a paste. Dissolve bouillon cubes in boiling water, and add this slowly to the flour mixture, stirring constantly to make gravy. • Mix in the onion, paprika, parsley, Worcestershire sauce to taste, and catsup. Simmer for 5 minutes. • Add lamb cubes, cover, and simmer for 10 minutes. Serve hot over rice.

Charles M. Duke, Jr.

On the Apollo 16 mission to what scientists believe to be the oldest area on the moon—the lunar highlands of the Descartes region—Charles Duke became the tenth man to walk on the moon. Among the scientific experiments performed, the first astronomical observation from a heavenly body other than the earth was made through an ultraviolet camera/spectroscope. As Duke is a native of South Carolina, his wife made a special request to space program officials that his breakfast on the moon include a healthy serving of grits. Duke resigned from the National Aeronautics and Space Administration and the Air Force in 1976 to join the Orbit Corporation. He is now in private business in San Antonio, Texas. *Recipe and comments from Charles M. Duke, Jr.*

Lunar Bread Makes 1 loaf

This recipe won first place in the celebrity division of the second annual world championship cornbread cookoff at Lockhart, Texas, and was developed by a good friend, Murray Denton.

¾ cup cornmeal
½ cup self-rising flour
1 cup diced ham
12 ounces Monterey Jack cheese with jalapeños, diced
12 ounces cottage cheese
6 eggs, beaten

• Blend all ingredients together thoroughly. Place in a greased cast-iron skillet and bake at 350° for 1 hour.

Donn F. Eisele

Greetings from the "lovely Apollo room, high atop every-thing" was a message to earth from the Apollo 7 mission in 1968. Donn Eisele served as command-module pilot for this first manned mission after the disastrous Apollo 1 fire. Apollo 7 was also the first manned earth-orbital test flight of the Apollo spacecraft. In 1972 Eisele became director of the Peace Corps in Thailand. He is currently with Marion Power Shovel Company in Williamsburg, Virginia. *Recipe and comments from Donn F. Eisele*

Mongolian Hot Pot   Serves 8

This is a wonderful way to entertain guests, with the meal being the evening's entertainment. The guests look forward to each change of ingre-dient and by the time the noodles are cooked the sauce is delicious from all of the other items cooked in it. We found our Oriental Hot Pot in Bangkok, and it is a cherished possession.

1 pound shrimp in shell
4 chicken breasts
1 pound beef sirloin or tenderloin
1 head cabbage
fresh bean sprouts
4 quarts chicken stock
rice noodles or glass noodles

Sauce
soy sauce
sesame oil
red chili pepper
Mix together to taste

• Shell and devein shrimp; bone chicken. Cut both chicken and beef into bite-size pieces. Coarsely chop the cabbage. Arrange all on a platter with bean sprouts. • Heat the stock in an electric pot or Oriental Hot Pot at the table. Using a slotted spoon or chopsticks, host cooks each item in stock separately to desired doneness and passes it to each guest, who in turn dips it in the sauce. • Cook noodles last, add remaining sauce, and ladle into bowls.

Richard F. Gordon, Jr.

As well as being an astronaut, Richard Gordon was also the 1961 winner of the Bendix Trophy Race, setting a new speed record of 869.74 miles per hour and a transcontinental speed record of 2 hours and 47 minutes. Gordon walked in space as pilot of the Gemini 11 mission, and was command-module pilot for Apollo 12 in 1969. He retired from the National Aeronautics and Space Administration and the navy to become executive vice president for the New Orleans Saints, and is now with the John Mecom Company. *Recipes and comments from Richard F. Gordon, Jr.*

Crêpes with Orange Sauce   Serves 8

This makes tons of crêpes, but they go quickly and everyone wants five or six of them. Can be made in advance—good for a Sunday breakfast or for dessert.

12 eggs
6 cups milk
2 scant cups flour
1¼ teaspoons salt
⅓ cup sugar
● Mix all crêpe ingredients in blender and let stand for about 1 hour. Make very thin pancakes in a crêpe pan. Roll up and pour sauce over crêpes.

Sauce
1 cup sugar
2 tablespoons cornstarch
¼ teaspoon salt
2 cups orange juice
4 tablespoons butter

● Mix cornstarch with a little orange juice until dissolved; add rest of ingredients and cook until moderately thick.

Gazpacho Serves 3-4

1 cube beef bouillon
½ cup hot water
12 ounces tomato juice
1 large ripe tomato,
  chopped
3 tablespoons finely
  chopped scallions
2 tablespoons finely
  chopped green pepper

¼ cup finely chopped
  cucumber
2 tablespoons red wine
  vinegar
1 teaspoon Worcestershire
  sauce
⅛ teaspoon Tabasco
salt and pepper to taste

Garnish

chopped green pepper, onion, tomato, cucumber
½ to 1 cup garlic-flavored croutons

• Dissolve bouillon cube in hot water. • Put all ingredients in blender and process until smooth. Place in freezer until cold and slushy. Blend again just before serving. • Garnish and serve cold in chilled bowls or balloon goblets.

James B. Irwin

As the eighth man to walk on the moon during the Apollo 15 mission in 1971, James Irwin was also one of the first to ride on it. Looking like a stripped-down version of a dune buggy, the Lunar Roving Vehicle allowed the astronauts to explore more of the surface of the moon than ever before. Irwin formed the High Flight Foundation in 1972, a evangelical-oriented organization, of which he is president. *Recipe from James B. Irwin*

Cream of Celery Soup   Serves 8

2 quarts homemade beef or chicken stock, strained (or 8 cups canned broth)
2 small bunches celery, diced
1 medium onion, chopped
½ pound butter
1 cup heavy cream
salt to taste
1 or 2 potatoes, diced (optional)

• Add the celery, onion, butter, and cream to the stock. Simmer until celery is soft. If soup is too thin, add 1 or 2 diced potatoes and cook until potatoes are soft. • Purée in batches in blender. Salt to taste. Can be served hot or cold.

James A. Lovell, Jr.

James Lovell is a seasoned veteran of many of the National Aeronautics and Space Administration's missions. His first experience in space was as pilot of Gemini 7, making the first spacecraft rendezvous with Gemini 6. He then became command-module pilot of Gemini 12, the link between the orbiting missions and the Apollo lunar landings. Later, he flew on Apollo 8, the first mission to orbit the moon. He was also commander of Apollo 13. In 1971, he became deputy director of science and application at the Johnson Space Center, and is now president of Fisk Telephone Systems in Houston, Texas. *Recipes and comments from James Lovell, Jr.*

Baked Tomatoes Rockefeller Serves 6

NASA should make this in a freeze-dried pack!

2 packages frozen chopped spinach	¼ teaspoon fresh garlic, minced
2 cups plain bread crumbs	½ teaspoon pepper
6 chopped green onions	1 teaspoon thyme
6 eggs slightly beaten	1 teaspoon seasoning salt
¾ cup melted butter	¼ teaspoon Tabasco
¼ cup Parmesan cheese	6 fresh ripe tomatoes, cut in half
1 teaspoon salt	

• Cook spinach according to package directions and drain well. Mix with all other ingredients except tomatoes.
• Arrange tomato halves in a single layer in a buttered baking dish. Mound spinach topping on tomatoes. • Cover and bake at 350° for about 25 minutes. Delicious with all meats, especially beef; it is also a nice buffet dish. The topping freezes well.

Dill Dip Serves 6-8

Great for dipping when discussing the next moon mission!

⅔ cup sour cream
⅔ cup mayonnaise
1 teaspoon dried dill weed
1 teaspoon Beau Monde seasoning
1 tablespoon dried parsley flakes
1 tablespoon thinly sliced green onions or scallions

• Mix first six ingredients together in order listed. Cover and chill. Serve with raw vegetable tray for cocktail hour.

Edgar D. Mitchell

Edgar Mitchell was the lunar-module pilot for Apollo 14 and the sixth man to walk on the moon. In 1972 he founded the Institute of Noetic Sciences, an organization dealing with research concerning health and human development, of which he is the chairman, and has published a book *Psychic Exploration: a Challenge for Science*. He is also president of the Edgar Mitchell Corporation. *Recipe from Mrs. Edgar D. Mitchell*

Country Spareribs   Serves 6

5 to 6 pounds of country-style spareribs
garlic powder
1 to 2 cups barbecue sauce
4 medium onions
Worcestershire sauce
1 lemon, thinly sliced

• Generously sprinkle the ribs with garlic powder. Place in a baking pan and cover with barbecue sauce. • Slice the onions and place them on top of the ribs. Shake Worcestershire sauce over all. • Place in a 350° oven and cook for ½ hour, basting frequently and adding more sauce as needed. • Lay sliced lemon over the meat, and cook until tender, about another 1½ hours. Serve with a tossed lettuce and watercress salad, corn on the cob, and cornbread with honey.

Harrison H. Schmitt

Harrison Schmitt undergoes the final flight fit checkout of his spacesuit.

"Jack" Schmitt was the first geologist to visit the lunar surface and examine it on site. A graduate of the California Institute of Technology with a doctorate in geology from Harvard University, he became the twelfth man to walk on the moon as lunar-module pilot for Apollo 17 in 1972. Before his selection as an astronaut, he had been one of the astrogeologists with the United States Geological Survey who instructed astronauts during their preflight geological training sessions. In 1974 Schmitt was named assistant administrator for energy programs of the National Aeronautics and Space Administration, and in 1976 he was elected to the United States Senate from his home state of New Mexico. *Recipe from Harrison H. Schmitt*

Schmitt's Special Chili   Serves 4

1 pound lean ground beef or pork
rosemary
sage
coarsely ground black pepper
1 cup cooked whole frijoles and juice
1 pint fresh (or canned) chili paste
1 large tomato
1 large onion
1 large sweet pepper
1 green chili
salt

• Sauté ground beef or pork and season to taste with rosemary, sage, and pepper. • Simmer together chili paste and frijoles, and add to meat mixture. • Coarsely chop vegetables and green chili, add to meat mixture, and cook over low heat for about 1 hour, stirring from time to time. Add salt to taste. Serve immediately with fresh tostados or corn chips.

Donald K. Slayton

Deke Slayton in the hatch between the Apollo Docking Module and the Soyuz Orbital Module.

Known as a "test pilot's test pilot," "Deke" Slayton was one of the first group of astronauts chosen in 1959. However, an erratic heart rate, later found to be inconsequential, prevented him from going into space for some time. He was director of Flight Crew Operations until 1974, when he was assigned to the Apollo/Soyuz Test Project as docking-module pilot. A major advance toward the international exploration of space, this mission was the first testing of a universal docking system and was a milestone in the development of rescue capabilities of astronauts and cosmonauts stranded in space. Slayton is now manager for Orbital Flight Tests for the Space Shuttle at the Johnson Space Center in Texas. *Recipe from Donald K. Slayton*

Chili

Serves 8

2 cups chopped onions
½ cup chopped celery
½ cup chopped green pepper
4 tablespoons salad oil
2 pounds round steak, ground
4 tablespoons chili powder
5 tablespoons cold water

4 cups canned tomatoes
2 cups tomato sauce
1½ teaspoons salt
½ teaspoon black pepper
4 teaspoons sugar
4 cloves garlic, minced
2 bay leaves
8 cups red beans, washed and soaked

• Sauté the onions, celery, and green pepper in salad oil in a large skillet. Add meat and brown. • Mix chili powder with water, and add to meat mixture. Stir in rest of the ingredients except the red beans. • Cook covered for 1 hour, then uncover and cook ½ hour. Add beans, cover, and simmer another 2 hours.

Thomas P. Stafford

The pilot of Gemini 6 and command pilot for Gemini 9, Thomas Stafford was selected commander for the critical Apollo 10 mission, which orbited the moon, testing various systems and examining the lunar surface in preparation for the first manned landing. He later commanded the Apollo/Soyuz Test Project. During this cooperative mission he acquired a taste for borscht, a Russian beet soup forming part of the rations of the Soyuz team. At one point as mission control queried the Soyuz on the problems of eating in space: "What about the borscht," to which the Soyuz responded: "Yes, we've prepared it . . . even three tubes for Tom."* In 1975 he became commander of Edwards Air Force Base in California. Stafford was chief of staff for Research and Development and Acquisitions of the Air Force until his retirement. *Recipes from Hazel Gecy, secretary to Thomas Stafford*

Rice with Green Chilies and Sour Cream   Serves 6

¾ cup rice
2 cups sour cream
½ pound Monterey Jack cheese, grated
salt
4 ounces diced green chilies
butter

Garnish
½ cup grated Monterey Jack cheese

• Cook rice according to package directions. Cool. • Mix in sour cream and cheese; salt to taste. Add diced chilies and mix well. • Place in casserole dish and top with the remaining cheese. Dot with butter. • Bake at 350° for approximately 20 minutes or until heated through and topping is melted. May be made ahead and refrigerated until needed.

---

*From "Stafford Finds Borscht Waiting Aboard Soyuz," The New York Times, July 18, 1975.

German Cream Cheese Brownies Makes 20

4 ounces German sweet chocolate

5 tablespoons butter

3 ounces cream cheese

1 cup sugar

4 eggs

½ cup flour

1½ teaspoons vanilla

½ teaspoon baking powder

¼ teaspoon salt

½ to 1 cup chopped walnuts

¼ teaspoon almond extract

• Preheat the oven to 350°. Grease a 9-inch-square baking pan. • Melt the chocolate with 3 tablespoons of the butter. Cool. • Cream together the remaining butter with the cream cheese and ¼ cup of the sugar until light and fluffy. Beat in 1 egg, 1 tablespoon of the flour, and ½ teaspoon of the vanilla. Set aside. • Beat the remaining 3 eggs until light and add the remaining sugar, flour, baking powder, and salt. Add the chocolate mixture, remaining vanilla, and almond extract. Measure out 1 cup of the chocolate batter and set aside. • Spread the remaining chocolate batter in pan and top with cheese batter. Drop reserved chocolate batter by tablespoons and swirl with a knife to marble. • Bake for 35 to 40 minutes. Cool before cutting. Wrap tightly to store in the refrigerator.

Chocolate Cheese Cake Serves 8-10

2 cups graham cracker crumbs (about 14 crackers)

½ cup butter or margarine, melted

1 cup plus 3 tablespoons sugar

1 envelope unflavored gelatin

¾ cup milk

¾ cup chocolate syrup

8 ounces cream cheese, softened

1½ teaspoons vanilla

1 cup whipping cream or 2 cups frozen nondairy whipped topping, defrosted

• Combine graham cracker crumbs, ⅓ cup of the sugar, and butter or margarine. Press mixture on the bottom and 1½ inches up the sides of a 9-inch springform pan or pie plate. Chill. • Mix ½ cup sugar and gelatin in a saucepan. Gradually add milk and chocolate syrup. Cook over medium heat, stirring constantly until sugar and gelatin dissolve. Cool. • In a small mixing bowl combine cream cheese, remaining sugar, and 1 tablespoon vanilla. Add chocolate mixture and blend thoroughly. Chill until mixture mounds slightly when dropped from a spoon. • Whip cream until slightly thickened; add ½ teaspoon vanilla and beat until stiff (if using whipped topping, stir in vanilla). Whip chocolate mixture for 30 seconds on medium speed of mixer. • Alternately spoon cream and chocolate mixture into the crust. Swirl with a spatula to give marbled effect. Chill several hours or overnight.

John L. Swigert, Jr.

When a prime crew member was exposed to measles, John Swigert became command-module pilot of Apollo 13, only 72 hours prior to launch. This lunar-landing mission became an ordeal of survival when a defective oxygen tank exploded, forcing the astronauts to use the lunar module as a lifeboat. Quick thinking and innovative action enabled them to orbit the moon and return home safely. In 1973 Swigert accepted a position as executive director of the Committee on Science and Technology of the House of Representatives, and in 1977 made a bid for the Senate seat from his native state of Colorado. *Recipes from Mrs. John L. Swigert, Sr.*

Jacksonville Crisps   Makes 2-3 dozen

½ cup butter or margarine
½ cup brown sugar, firmly packed
½ cup white sugar
1 egg, well beaten
¾ cup flour
½ teaspoon baking powder
⅛ teaspoon salt
1 teaspoon vanilla
¼ cup cornflakes
1 cup quick-cooking oats

• Preheat oven to 375°. Grease cookie sheet. • Cream shortening together with sugars until light and fluffy. Beat in egg. • Sift together flour, baking powder, and salt, and mix with batter. • Stir in vanilla, nuts, cornflakes, and oats. Mix well. • Drop rounded teaspoonfuls on cookie sheet and bake for 10 minutes.

Sweet and Sour Barbecued Ribs   Serves 4-5

2 pounds meaty country-style spareribs
1 small clove garlic (optional)
8 ounces tomato sauce
⅔ cup catsup
½ cup vinegar
1 cup pineapple juice
⅓ cup brown sugar
1 teaspoon dry mustard
2 tablespoons Worcestershire sauce

• Line a 9 × 13-inch pan with foil. Place ribs in a single layer in pan. • Broil on all sides until well browned. Drain off all grease. Wipe the pan with paper towels to remove residue, and replace ribs. • Combine all other ingredients in a saucepan and bring to a boil, stirring occasionally. Pour over ribs • Bake uncovered at 325° for 1½ hours or until sauce is absorbed by meat, basting several times. This sauce can also be used with pork chops or chicken.

ENGINEERS, INDUSTRIALISTS, AND OTHERS

Olive Ann Beech
Supper Nachos
Creamed Spinach

Chesley Bonestell
Brandy Manhattan

Joseph Charyk
German Pancake

Edgar M. Cortright
Crab Dip
Rolls

Kurt Heinrich Debus
Old-fashioned Sourdough Bread

Charles Dollfus
Canard à l'Orange

Hugh Latimer Dryden
Shrimp Spread
Phony Spumoni

Paul Garber
My Mother's Dutch Cake

Charles Harvard Gibbs-Smith
Toasted Welsh Rarebit

Edward Henry Heinemann
Key Lime Pie

Christopher C. Kraft, Jr.
Oysters Rockefeller

Jerome Lederer
Zwetschken Knödeln

Edwin A. Link
Conch Fritters

Alexander Lippisch
Stuffed Baked Tomatoes
Arroz con Pollo

Peter Lissaman
Caviar Oleg

Pierre Lissarrague
Coq au Vin

Paul B. MacReady
Fruit Spread

John McLucas
Aunt Donella's Birthday Cake Icing

Oran Nicks
Camp Omelet

John K. Northrop
Cottage Cheese Pancakes

Paul Poberezny
No-Peep Chicken

Dawson Ransome
Bran Muffins
Banana-Nut Bread

Francis M. Rogallo
Deviled Crabs
Raisin-Nut Pie

Lee R. Scherer
Magic Cookie Bars

Robert Seamans
Café Brûlot

Robert Six
Picadillo à la Six

Richard L. Uppstrom
Quiche Alsace Lorraine

Walter C. Williams
Hamburger Chili Rellenos
Crab Meat Sauté

Olive Ann Beech

The Beech Aircraft Corporation, founded by Walter Beech in the 1920s as Travel Air, today has become one of the most successful aircraft manufacturers in the country. Involved in the company since its inception, Mrs. Beech is now chairman of the board. Until recently, she was the only woman chief executive in the aircraft industry. In 1959 she was awarded the Paul Tissandier Diploma of the Fédération Aéronautique Internationale. *Recipes and comments from Olive Ann Beech*

Supper Nachos Serves 4-6

1 pound lean ground beef
1 large onion, chopped
1 or 2 pounds canned refried beans
4 ounces whole California green chilies or green chili sauce
2 to 3 cups shredded Monterey Jack or mild Cheddar
  cheese (or a combination of both)
¾ cup prepared green or red taco sauce

Garnish (any or all of the following)
¼ cup chopped green onions
1 cup pitted ripe olives
1 cup guacamole or ripe avocado, mashed
1 cup sour cream
1 mild red pickled pepper
fresh parsley sprigs

In the Travel Air days, Mr. Beech and the pilots wanted to teach me to fly. Their idea of instruction was to take me up and then stunt the airplane. In those days, you know, a plane was no good unless it flew upside down.

• Fry meat until brown and add salt and pepper to taste. Push meat to one side. Add onion and brown. • Spread one or two cans refried beans in a shallow 10 × 15-inch oval pan or oven-proof dish. Top evenly with meat and onions. • Chop 1 can green chilies and spread over meat. Cover evenly with shredded cheese and drizzle taco sauce over cheese. • Bake uncovered at 400° for 20 to 25 minutes, until cheese melts. Remove from oven and garnish with any or all of the items listed.

Serve with nachos, corn chips, tortillas, or tacos. If used as a main dish, serve with tossed salad. Good as an appetizer, but filling.

Creamed Spinach   Serves 6-8

8 pounds fresh leaf spinach or 8 10-ounce packages frozen
  chopped spinach
2 tablespoons butter
2 tablespoons flour
2 cups light cream or milk, warm
salt
nutmeg
white pepper

• Cook spinach in a small amount of water in a large pot,
with a plate or lid on top of spinach to weight it down.
Cook in 1- or 2-pound batches. Spinach will cook down to
about 8 cups. Drain and chop fine. For frozen spinach follow directions on package. • In a large saucepan, melt the
butter and add the flour. Whisk until smooth. Add the
cream or milk and cook over low heat until lightly thickened. • Add the spinach and season to taste with salt,
nutmeg, and white pepper. Put in oven-proof serving dish
and keep warm until served.

Chesley Bonestell

Chesley Bonestell in front of his 1957 concept of a moonscape.

Chesley Bonestell has imagined and illustrated, as well as witnessed, flight from the earth to the moon and beyond our solar system. Called the "Old Master of Space Art," he has illustrated many science-fiction stories and books, as well as created film-scene backgrounds as a special-effects artist for movies such as *War of the Worlds* and *When Worlds Collide,* depicting his own concepts of the far reaches of space. He also collaborated with Wernher Von Braun and Willy Ley on books such as *The Exploration of Mars. Recipe from Chesley Bonestell*

Brandy Manhattan   Serves 1

First, pile as much Camembert, Liederkranz, or Brie cheese on four crispy round crackers as they will hold. Then, into a tall glass pour 4 ounces of the best brandy and 2 ounces of sweet white vermouth over three ice-cubes. Now, imbibe the drink and enjoy the crackers.

The first glassful will relax you after the day's stress, the second will revive your spirits. A third, and you will experience a sensation of taking off into space with no need of technology nor any expense to the taxpayer. I have frequently resorted to this formula when traveling across the country at 40,000 feet and found that it seemed to shorten the time of a transcontinental trip.

Joseph Charyk

As president and director of Communications Satellite Corporation since 1963, Joseph Charyk was directly involved in the INTELSAT agreements of 1971, an international cooperative venture for worldwide satellite communications. At this time, he said: "In six years since little old 'Early Bird' . . . there are very few things that are better and cheaper. In this case, we have a dramatic demonstration—not only do we have communications all around the world that were unthinkable six years ago, they are better." As a professor of aeronautics at Princeton in the 1940s and 50s, he assisted in establishing the Guggenheim Jet Propulsion Center there. Prior to joining Communications Satellite Corporation, Charyk was associated with the Air Force as chief scientist and assistant secretary for research and development, and as under secretary. *Recipe from Joseph Charyk*

German Pancake

2 large servings

4 egg yolks
2 tablespoons cornstarch
1/3 cup milk
1/3 cup water
1 teaspoon salt

1 tablespoon powdered
 sugar
2 lemons
6 egg whites
1 tablespoon butter
extra powdered sugar for
 dusting

• Combine egg yolks with the cornstarch, milk, water, salt, sugar, and grated peel of lemons. Stir until creamy smooth. • Beat egg whites until stiff and fold into the batter. • Melt butter in skillet and pour in batter when skillet is hot. Reduce heat immediately and let cook for several minutes or until batter begins to firm. (If desired, a lemon filling with fresh grated rind may be added and pancake folded over it). Finally, sprinkle with extra powdered sugar and the juice of the 2 lemons.

Edgar M. Cortright

An authority on propulsion, Edgar Cortright has made fundamental contributions to the science of fluid dynamics. He began in 1948 as a research scientist in aerodynamics at the Lewis Flight Propulsion Center. In 1958 he became chief of advanced technical programs at the headquarters of the National Aeronautics and Space Administration, organizing the Tiros and Nimbus meteorological satellites. From 1960 to 1961 Cortright served as assistant director of lunar and planetary programs. After serving as a NASA deputy administrator with the Office of Space Science Applications and the Office of Manned Space Flight, he was named director of the Langley Research Center. He left the government in 1975 and is now president of the Lockheed–California Corporation. *Recipes and comments from Edgar M. Cortright*

Fortunate are those who have lived in the tidewater area of Virginia. The Chesapeake Bay blue crab is one of the reasons, and this is one of the many ways to enjoy this delicacy.

Crab Dip
Serves 8-10

1 pound crabmeat
½ cup chopped scallions
½ cup pickle relish
1 teaspoon salt
1 cup mayonnaise
½ cup sour cream

● Mix all ingredients together. Cover and refrigerate all day. Drain and serve with Melba toast.

Rolls
Makes approximately 6 dozen small rolls

1 yeast cake
¾ cup sugar
2 cups lukewarm water
1 teaspoon salt
⅔ cup melted shortening
2 eggs, beaten
6½ to 7 cups flour

● Crumble yeast in a bowl. Sprinkle sugar over it and let it sit for 15 minutes. ● Pour lukewarm water, salt, and melted shortening over the yeast, and stir in eggs. Add flour and knead until smooth. Cover and let rise in a warm, draft-free place, until double in bulk (about 1½ hours). ● Punch down and let rise again. ● Shape into rolls and let rise for the third time. Bake at 350° for about 15 minutes. Do not overbrown. Rolls can be half baked, frozen, and when needed the baking can be finished.

Kurt Heinrich Debus

Kurt Debus began his long astronautics career as a rocket test engineer at Peenemünde, the wartime German rocket research center. In 1945 he joined his colleagues in immigrating to the United States where he served in a number of key positions with the Army Ballistic Missile Agency. Named first director of the National Aeronautics and Space Administration facility at Cape Canaveral in 1958, Debus was responsible for the administration of the Kennedy Space Center and supervised the launch of virtually every NASA mission prior to his retirement in 1975. He is now chairman of the board of directors of OTRAG, a European firm that hopes to develop a relatively low-cost space launch system. *Recipe from Kurt H. Debus*

Old-fashioned Sourdough Bread Makes 3 large loaves*

Sourdough Starter
1 package dry yeast
1 cup lukewarm water
1½ teaspoons salt
2½ cups white flour

• Dissolve yeast in water. Add salt and mix thoroughly with flour to make a smooth dough. Cover and let rise until double in bulk. • Punch dough down and place in a covered container twice the size of the amount of dough as it will expand. Refrigerate for about a week. This makes approximately 3 cups of starter.

Sourdough Bread
3 cups sourdough starter
2½ pounds white flour (about 10 cups sifted)
2½ pounds whole wheat or rye flour (about 10 cups sifted)
2 packages dry yeast
lukewarm water
salt to taste (about ½ handful)

Editor's note: This recipe can be cut in half to make 2 small loaves.

Kurt Debus stands inside the Vehicle Assembly Building at the Kennedy Space Center.

• Remove the sourdough starter from refrigerator and bring to room temperature. • Dissolve the yeast in 2 cups lukewarm water. Mix into 5 to 6 cups of the white flour to make a soft dough and let rise for about 1 hour. • Stir together the remaining flour, and add lukewarm water (about 3 cups) a few tablespoons at a time, until all flour is dampened. Knead in the sourdough starter and yeast dough until well mixed, adding more flour or water if needed to create a smooth dough that comes loose from hands and dish. Cover and let rise until double in bulk, about 1½ hours. • Knead again for about 10 minutes. In order to provide sourdough for the next baking, remove three cups of the dough and place in a covered container twice the size of the amount of dough. Refrigerate. • Cut remaining dough into three equal parts and place in Teflon or well-greased loaf pans. Let the dough rise until it fills the pans, about 2 hours. • Bake at 350° for 1 hour, or until brown. The bread will have a thick crust. The loaves freeze well if wrapped in foil shortly after they have cooled.

Charles Dollfus

Octogenarian Dollfus has made over 500 gas and hot-air balloon ascensions in his lifetime. His first solo balloon ascent at the age of twenty was made in 1913; the following year he unintentionally crossed the English Channel from France and landed in Wales. Fifty years later the famous French aeronaut crossed the Alps with his friend Jan Boesman in their balloon *Toberlerone,* and Dollfus acknowledged that "our Alps crossing was the most beautiful balloon flight of my life." Founder of the French Musée de l'Air in Paris, Dollfus served as its curator for over 30 years, and coauthored with Henri Bouche the flight-history classic, *Histoire de l'Aeronautique. Recipe supplied by his friend, Pierre Lissarrague*

Canard à l'Orange (Braised Duck with Orange Sauce) Serves 6

1 6-pound duck
salt and pepper
4 tablespoons butter
2 oranges, peeled and
  quartered
1½ teaspoons dried orange
  peel

2 cups traditional French
  brown stock (canned beef
  consommé can be used)
½ cup dry white wine
1 teaspoon cornstarch
  mixed with ½ cup cold
  water (optional)

• Prepare duck for cooking; season cavity with salt and pepper. • Brown duck in butter in heavy pan; place breast side up. • Add dried peel and stock; *cover pan tightly* and simmer until tender, about 1½ hours. • Remove duck, and keep warm. • Skim fat from stock and remove all but ½ cup. • Add wine and heat to boiling point. (Optional: to thicken sauce add cornstarch mixed with cold water.) • Place duck on platter; pour sauce over it and garnish with orange.

Hugh Latimer Dryden

1898–1965

A highly creative and imaginative engineer/administrator, Hugh Dryden was fond of remarking that "the airplane and I grew up together." He began his career as a physicist with the National Bureau of Standards in 1919; over the next two decades he became a leader of aerodynamic research in the United States. He was named director of the National Advisory Committee for Aeronautics and in 1958 became deputy director of the new National Aeronautics and Space Administration. Dryden was the recipient of virtually every major achievement award in his field.
Recipes from Mrs. Hugh L. Dryden

Shrimp Spread   Makes approximately 1 cup
4½ ounces cooked, deveined shrimp
¾ teaspoon "Old Bay Spice"
¾ teaspoon celery seed
6 tablespoons sour cream
assorted crackers or celery stalks

• Rinse shrimp three or four times. Mince very fine. • Mix shrimp with spice and celery seed. Toss with sour cream. • To store in refrigerator, place in a tightly capped glass container. Serve spread on crackers or stuff celery with the mixture.

Phony Spumoni   Serves 6-8
2-ounce package dessert topping mix
⅓-cup quartered red maraschino cherries
1 tablespoon chopped candied orange peel
1 tablespoon chopped toasted almonds
1 quart rich vanilla ice cream

• Prepare dessert topping mix according to package directions. Fold in cherries, orange peel, and almonds; refrigerate until ready to use. • Scoop ice cream into a bowl; stir to soften slightly. Press ice cream on bottom and sides of a 6-cup mold or a foil-lined loaf dish, forming a uniform shell. • Working quickly, spoon cream mixture into center. • Cover and freeze 6 to 8 hours or overnight. • To unmold, press a hot, damp towel closely around mold until ice cream slides out.

Paul E. Garber

Paul Garber in 1950 with the target kite he invented for the navy in 1942.

As a young curator, Paul Garber presumed to suggest to the Secretary of the Smithsonian Institution that a cable be sent to Charles Lindbergh, congratulating him on a successful flight before Lindbergh landed in Paris—for he was certain that Lindbergh would make it. Later, Garber was instrumental in the acquisition of the *Spirit of St. Louis* for the Smithsonian, where it has been on exhibit since 1928. This was the beginning of a lifelong campaign to save numerous historical aircraft, including the Wright brothers 1903 machine. The Preservation, Restoration, and Storage Facility of the National Air and Space Museum has recently been named the Paul E. Garber Facility in his honor. Now historian emeritus at the museum, Garber has never forgotten his first love, the kite. Every March he teaches the fun of kite making, and conducts the kite-flying competition at the Smithsonian Kite Festival. *Recipe from Mrs. Paul Garber*

My Mother's Dutch Cake

Makes 1 loaf

½ cup shortening
1 cup sugar
2 eggs
1 teaspoon vanilla
1½ cups cake flour
2 teaspoons baking powder
½ teaspoon salt
¼ cup raisins, chopped
¼ cup citron, chopped
¼ cup candied cherries, chopped
pinch of ground cloves
½ cup milk.

• Cream the shortening, gradually adding the sugar. • Beat eggs until light. Add, with vanilla, to the shortening. Beat until creamy. • Sift together flour, baking powder, and salt. Mix into this the raisins, citron, cherries, and cloves. Stir into batter, alternating with the milk. • Bake in a greased and floured loaf pan at 350° for 45 minutes or until brown and firm in the center.

Charles Harvard Gibbs-Smith

One of the world's foremost historians of flight, Charles Gibbs-Smith is also considered by many in the aviation field to be the leading authority on the Wright brothers. He is a Keeper Emeritus of the Victoria and Albert Museum and a research fellow of the Science Museum in London. Dr. Gibbs-Smith was the first occupant, in 1978, of the Charles A. Lindbergh Chair of Aerospace History at the National Air and Space Museum, an honor offered to outstanding scholars in the fields of aviation or space history. *Recipe and comments from Charles Harvard Gibbs-Smith*

Toasted Welsh Rarebit   Serves 4

I am a vegetarian. When I was a child after World War I, meat was scarce and thus what was available was frequently unappetizing, so I never really acquired a taste for it.

1 pound English Cheddar cheese, grated
½ cup beer
1 teaspoon mustard
1 teaspoon Worcestershire sauce
4 slices white bread, toasted

• Place cheese in a saucepan over low heat. Stir in beer while the cheese melts. Add mustard and Worcestershire sauce. • Pour cheese mixture on toast and place under broiler until the cheese starts to brown.

Edward Henry Heinemann

Edward Heinemann after his first flight in the A-4 Skyhawk, almost twenty years after he designed it.

A legend among aeronautical engineers, Edward Heinemann began his career with the Moreland Aircraft Corporation in 1931, and retired in 1962 as a vice president of the General Dynamics Corporation. During this time he amassed an extraordinary list of design credits. Perhaps his most famous design is the versatile Douglas A-4 Skyhawk, known as "Heinemann's Hotrod." The A-4 first flew in 1954 and is still operational today. *Recipe and comments from Edward H. Heinemann*

Key Lime Pie Serves 6

To me, no meal is complete without dessert! Key Lime Pie apparently originated in Florida. It is a very fine dessert for hot weather especially, and is liked by almost everyone.

4 eggs, separated
14 ounces sweetened condensed milk
½ cup lime juice
2 or 3 teaspoons grated lime peel
few drops green food coloring (optional)
9-inch pie shell, baked
½ teaspoon cream of tartar
½ cup sugar

• Beat egg yolks. Stir in milk, lime juice, grated peel, and food coloring. • Beat 1 egg white until stiff, and fold into milk mixture. Turn into pastry shell. • Beat reserved egg whites with cream of tartar until foamy; gradually add sugar, beating until stiff but not dry. Spread meringue on top of pie, sealing carefully to edge of shell. • Bake at 350° for 15 minutes, or until meringue is golden brown. Chill before serving.

Christopher C. Kraft, Jr.

Selected as one of the original members of the National Aeronautics and Space Administration's Space Task Group in 1958, Chris Kraft was a prime contributor to the development of many of the basic mission- and flight-control techniques. He was flight director for all of the Mercury missions and many of the Gemini, and directed the design and implementation of the Mission Control Center in Houston. Since 1972 he has been director of the Johnson Space Center. *Recipe from Christopher C. Kraft, Jr.*

Oysters Rockefeller   Serves 10

1 large onion, minced
4 bay leaves, crumbled
1 teaspoon celery salt
1 teaspoon salt
¼ teaspoon cayenne
2 packages frozen chopped spinach (do not cook, just thaw and drain)
2 tablespoons parsley, minced
2 teaspoons Worcestershire sauce
1 pound butter
1 cup cracker meal
6 tablespoons sherry wine
1½ quarts shucked oysters
1 cup grated Parmesan cheese
1 cup bread crumbs
lemon wedges

• In a large bowl combine onion, bay leaves, celery salt, salt, cayenne, chopped spinach, parsley, and Worcestershire sauce. Mix thoroughly. • Melt butter in a saucepan over low flame. Remove from heat, combine with cracker meal and sherry wine, and mix thoroughly. Add to mixture in bowl and combine well. • Place oysters in two 3-quart oblong casseroles. Pour mixture over oysters and sprinkle with Parmesan cheese and bread crumbs. • Bake in a preheated 400° oven for *only* 10 minutes. Overcooking will toughen the oysters. Serve with lemon wedges. (Cook one casserole at a time for your guests so the oysters will be hot and will not be overcooked).

This is delicious served with spoon bread and a tossed salad. Cherries Jubilee for dessert!

Jerome Lederer

An authority on air and space flight safety, Jerome Lederer began as an aeronautical engineer with the United States Air Mail Service in 1926. He later established and directed the Safety Bureau of the Civil Aeronautics Board, and directed the training of 10,000 pilots in World War II. In 1947 Lederer headed the Flight Safety Foundation when it was formed, and from 1967 to 1972 he was director of safety in the Office of Manned Space Flight of the National Aeronautics and Space Administration. He is currently the president of the Air Mail Pioneers. *Recipe and comments from Jerome Lederer*

Zwetschken Knödeln   Serves 4

In my youth, I spent the entire three months of every summer with a small group of friends canoeing, running rapids, and camping in the then-uncharted wilds of northern Quebec. On one trip I was pursued by the Royal Canadian Mounted Police— mounted in canoes! We enjoyed delicious repasts of freshly caught fish, often followed by a wonderful dessert of blueberry pie made from berries freshly plucked from the vines along the riverbank. My mother would welcome us home at the end of the summer with these apricot dumplings, an Austrian peasant dessert literally glowing with robust, tangy flavor.

2 tablespoons butter
1¼ cups water
1¼ cups flour
dash salt
2 eggs
1½ pounds apricots or plums
½ cup white bread crumbs
½ cup sugar

● Heat 1½ tablespoons of the butter in a saucepan with the water. Add flour and salt all at once and stir vigorously until mixture no longer sticks to spoon and pan. Remove from heat and cool slightly. ● Add eggs, one at a time, beating until each is well blended. Form into a thick roll, about 5 inches in diameter, and chill. ● Wipe fruit with a dry towel. If fruit is very tart, remove pits and place a cube of sugar in the center; or leave whole. ● Slice roll thinly and wrap each fruit in a piece of dough, sealing the edges well. ● Fill a deep saucepan half full of water and add a sprinkle of salt. Bring water to a slow boil and cook the dumplings, a few at a time, for 5 minutes each. Remove with a slotted spoon and drain on paper towels. ● Fry bread crumbs in remaining butter until yellow. Roll the dumplings in the fried crumbs and sprinkle with sugar. Serve hot.

Edwin A. Link

Although best known for his development in 1929 of the Link Flight Trainer, Ed Link is the holder of over thirty patents in the fields of aviation and ocean engineering. During World War II, the Link Trainer was used to teach flying to more than half a million airmen throughout the world. He established the Link Foundation in 1953 to support research in both aeronautics and oceanology. Since the early 1950s, Mr. Link has been involved with his second career—that of underwater research and archeology. He designed the oceanographic research vessel, *Sea Diver,* from which his ingenious lock-out submersibles are launched. Currently, he helps direct an unusual oceanographic center, the Harbor Branch Foundation, Inc., near Fort Pierce, Florida. Among the many honors and awards that have been bestowed upon Mr. Link, the most recent is the 1980 Lindbergh Award for a half century of innovation in the fields of aviation and underwater exploration. *Recipe from Harbor Branch Foundation, Inc.*

Conch Fritters   Makes approximately 72

This recipe for Conch Fritters is a favorite of my brother's. It is the concoction of John Margetis, Ed and Marion Link's long-time chef aboard the Sea Diver. *With such good cooks as his wife Marion and John Margetis, Ed enjoys eating what they prepare. He is, however, still the primary chef for charcoal broiled steaks over his own indoor grill in Florida.—Marylyn C. Link*

3 pounds frozen conch, thawed and cleaned
3 large green peppers
3 large onions
1 stalk celery
3 teaspoons salt
¼ teaspoon oregano
2 teaspoons garlic salt
1 teaspoon Italian seasoning
1 teaspoon paprika
¼ teaspoon Tabasco
3 cups flour, sifted
6 teaspoons baking powder
3 cups cold milk
oil for frying

● Grind conch fine. Grind onions, green peppers, and celery. Add seasonings and mix well. Place in refrigerator for about ½ hour. Add 3 cups sifted flour mixed with baking powder and cold milk. Mix thoroughly. ● Heat 1 quart cooking oil in a 9″ frying pan, adding ½ cup olive oil if desired. When hot, dip a teaspoon in hot oil, then drop one teaspoon of batter into oil. Turn gently until brown; about 2 minutes. Make a dozen at a time. Remove and drop on brown paper. Serve hot with cocktail sauce or mustard.

Alexander Lippisch
1894–1976

After seeing a demonstration flight in 1909 by Orville Wright at Tempelhof, a suburb of Berlin, Alexander Lippisch rushed home to build a model of the plane, and then to construct several of his own design. He continued to design planes and after World War I worked on sailplanes and gliders until 1939. The inventor of the delta wing used in high-speed aircraft, he was the chief of design and speed research for the Messerschmitt company and developed the first operational rocket-powered fighter plane, the ME 163 B. Later, he was made director of research at the Airplane Research Institute in Vienna. At the end of World War II, he came to the United States to work for the technical intelligence section of the Air Force. In 1957 he entered private industry and at the time of his death was developing an airfoil boat and an aerodyne, a wingless aircraft, for West Germany. *Recipes and comments from Mrs. Alexander Lippisch*

Alexander's father was an artist and when he was newly married he obtained a stipend to work in Rome. There Alexander's mother learned to cook many Italian dishes using tomatoes which at the time were little known in Germany and even considered poisonous by some people. . . . when tomatoes were in season, I could always make Alexander happy with a dish of baked tomatoes with rice filling for which his mother had given me the recipe.

Stuffed Baked Tomatoes   Serves 6

6 medium tomatoes
6 tablespoons converted rice
6 teaspoons peanut oil
salt
chopped parsley

• Cut the tops off of the tomatoes, and scoop out the pulp, being careful not to pierce the shell. Put the pulp and juice through a sieve to remove the seeds. • Into each tomato put one tablespoon of rice and one teaspoon of oil. Fill up the shell with the reserved pulp and juice, sprinkle with salt, and replace the caps. • Place in a greased baking dish and bake at 350° for 45-50 minutes or until tomatoes are soft and rice is cooked. Garnish with parsley.

Arroz con Pollo

Serves 4-6

1 frying chicken
3 to 4 tablespoons oil
3 onions, chopped
¼ pound ham, diced
2 medium tomatoes,
  chopped
3 sweet red peppers,
  chopped

1 cup rice
3 cups chicken stock
salt
pepper
minced parsley

• Cut the chicken into serving pieces. Heat oil in a large frying pan and sauté the pieces until lightly golden. • Add the onion, ham, tomatoes, and red pepper. Stir over heat for a few minutes and add the rice. Cook until rice browns. • Add the stock and cover. Turn heat to low and cook about 25 minutes, or until rice is done. Salt and pepper to taste and garnish with parsley. Serve with peas or asparagus tips.

Peter Lissaman

Since the disastrous flight of Icarus, human-powered flight has remained an unattainable goal. However, on August 23, 1977, this oldest aviation dream was fulfilled in the 7½-minute flight of the *Gossamer Condor,* a craft of aluminium tubes and transparent plastic powered by a bicycle apparatus. Dr. Lissaman designed the airfoil sections and propeller of the *Gossamer Condor* as a member of Paul MacCready's team. An aerodynamicist and designer, Lissaman has contributed to the design of sailboats, gliders, and road vehicles as well as airplanes. He is currently a vice president of AeroVironment Inc., of California, exploring alternate energy systems. *Recipe and comments from Peter Lissaman*

My first taste of aviation, and of caviar, was at the flying club of my hometown in Durban, Africa. The aircraft were mainly the lovely de Havilland biplanes of that period—Moths of all varieties, including a Leopard owned by my father. The club secretary, operations officer, barman, and cook, was an expatriate Russian aristocrat, Oleg, who claimed to be a grand duke. The duchess Sonya, equally improbably, ran the kitchen, served, and washed dishes.

There was a grass field, and on Saturdays the members reclined in deck chairs on the green unkempt lawn outside the hangar. The biplanes wheeled like clockwork toys in the warm breeze off the Indian Ocean; and with grand style, Oleg would serve the caviar and champagne as the golden afternoon faded. A year later the Hitler war came, my father was recalled to the service, and those sunlit colonial afternoons ended forever.

Caviar Oleg

Serves 2-4

1 cup mayonnaise
  (preferably homemade)
1 tablespoon red wine
  vinegar
juice of ½ of a lemon
2 tablespoons
  Worcestershire sauce
2 teaspoons whole celery
  seed
pinch of paprika

½ medium-size red onion
4 hard-boiled egg yolks
pepper to taste
2 teaspoons capers
4 small lemons
4 ounces caviar
4 ounces unsalted wafer
  crackers (such as
  Bremner's)

• Mix together the mayonnaise, vinegar, lemon juice, and Worcestershire sauce, stirring to form a smooth dressing. Add the celery seed. Place in a dish and set inside a larger bowl filled with ice and sprinkle with the paprika. • Mince the onion and place in a small serving dish. Chop the egg yolks, season with pepper, and place in another dish and garnish with capers. • Cut the lemons into wedges. Place caviar in one more dish on a bed of ice, and garnish with the lemons. To serve, spread a cracker with dressing, smother with caviar and onion, top with egg yolk, and squeeze lemon on top.

Definitely to be washed down with good cold extra-dry champagne, in those tall slender flutes. Serves two or four, depending upon what events follow.

Pierre Lissarrague

Général Pierre Lissarrague was a bomber pilot during World War II and participated in the war in French Indochina in the mid-fifties. During his military career, he was air attaché to the embassy of France in Madrid, Spain. In a civilian capacity, he currently directs the Musée de l'Air et de l'Espace in Paris which portrays the development of French aeronautical design with prototype aircraft from Mirages to the Concorde. *Recipe from Pierre Lissarrague*

Coq au Vin (Chicken with Wine) Serves 6

20 small whole onions
3½ ounces ham, diced
2 tablespoons butter
2 tablespoons cooking oil
salt and pepper
5-pound chicken, cut into
  serving pieces
½ cup brandy or Cognac
1 tablespoon flour
¾ bottle red Bordeaux (St.
  Emilion or Pomerol
suggested) or red
  Burgundy
2 tablespoons garlic, minced
10 small mushrooms,
  thoroughly cleaned
1 bay leaf
½ teaspoon thyme
1 teaspoon rosemary
5 cubes sugar
1 truffle, diced (optional)

• Brown onions and ham in a skillet with butter and 1 tablespoon cooking oil. Remove and reserve. • Sprinkle chicken with salt and pepper, and brown in a Dutch oven or heavy stock pot with remaining tablespoon oil. Remove from heat. Pour over brandy or Cognac and ignite, averting face. Shake pan gently until flames disappear. • Add onions and ham to chicken and sprinkle with flour. Warm wine in a saucepan and pour over; add garlic, mushrooms, bay leaf, thyme, rosemary, sugar cubes, and truffle. Cover and simmer over low heat approximately 1 hour, or until chicken is cooked. • Arrange chicken, onions, and mushrooms on a serving platter. Skim fat from sauce, strain, and pour over chicken. Platter may be garnished with thin slices of French bread browned in butter.

Paul B. MacCready

The Gossamer Condor *in flight.*

Creator of the human-powered *Gossamer Condor* and *Albatross* aircraft, Dr. MacCready has also worked in such diverse fields as sailplane development, meteorology, cloud-seeding, and atmospheric environment activities. He learned to fly as a navy pilot during World War II and earned a degree in physics at Yale in 1947, when his interest turned from powered aircraft to gliders. In 1948, 1949, and 1953, he won the National Soaring Championships, pioneering high-altitude wave soaring, and in 1956 became the first American to win the International Soaring Championship. MacCready conceived the *Gossamer Condor* in 1976, and in 1977 it won the Kremer prize for the first controlled, sustained, human-powered flight. Developing the concept further, the *Gossamer Albatross* became the first human-powered craft to fly the English Channel. Dr. MacCready is currently the president of AeroVironment, Inc., of Pasadena, California, which he founded in 1970. The company provides services and research in the study of energy and the environment. *Recipe from Dr. Joseph A. Mastropaolo, exercise physiologist for the* Gossamer Condor *and* Albatross *projects*

Diet and training of the pilot is a vital factor in the success of human-powered flight. This recipe is used on bread instead of butter or jelly, or as a pie filling, and quantitatively reduces calories, fat, sugar, and sodium. The atmosphere as the last athletic frontier has been penetrated at last, and I expect to witness thousands flying by their own power before the year 2000—extending their lives and avoiding degenerative disorders in the process.—Dr. Joseph A. Mastropaolo

Fruit Spread   Makes 5¼ cups

2 29-ounce cans sliced
  peaches, drained
1 20-ounce can crushed
  pineapple in *own* juice,
  drained
¼ teaspoon cinnamon

• Place drained peaches in blender set on coarse, turning machine on and off to obtain a coarse texture; remove and reserve. • Repeat with drained pineapple. • Mix the two fruits well and add cinnamon. • Can be served on bread, toast, French toast, or pancakes. • To store, refrigerate in a covered container.

John McLucas

Dr. McLucas was undersecretary of the Air Force from 1969 to 1963 when he was appointed secretary, a position he held until 1975, at which time he became administrator of the Federal Aviation Commission. His association with COMSAT General Corporation began in 1977 where he is currently executive vice president for International Communications and Technical Services. Active in private industry at various times, he holds ten United States patents. *Recipe and comments from John McLucas*

Aunt Donella's Birthday Cake Icing   Ices 1 cake

As a child I moved around from one family to another. Then at the age of 10, I finally moved into the home of Uncle Harold and Aunt Donella. Shortly thereafter, I had a birthday and she served a beautiful yellow cake with this bitter chocolate icing. I knew I had finally found a real home.

3 cups sugar
scant ½ cup light corn syrup
½ cup water
7 ounces baking chocolate
2 or 3 tablespoons butter or margarine
1 teaspoon vanilla

• Mix sugar, corn syrup, and water in a very large skillet. • Melt chocolate in a double boiler and add to sugar mixture. Add butter, and boil to the soft-ball stage. Cool. • Stir in vanilla. Beat to a good spreading consistency. If the icing gets too hard, add a drop or two of boiling water. Makes enough to frost between two or three layers, top, and sides of a 9-inch cake.

Oran Nicks

Deputy director of the National Aeronautics and Space Administration's Langley Research Center since 1970, Oran Nicks is also interested in the sport of sailplaning. He is president of the Tidewater Soaring Society which supports research and development activities in behalf of soaring. Nicks held engineering and management positions with North American Aviation and Chance Vought Aircraft before joining the National Aeronautics and Space Administration in 1960. For ten years he was responsible for such unmanned lunar and planetary programs as Ranger, Surveyor, Mariner, and Pioneer, as well as other space sciences, applications, and research and technology programs. *Recipe and comments from Oran Nicks*

Camp Omelet   Serves 4

Served with camp toast or bread, this quickly prepared breakfast will satisfy four hungry campers with a minimum of equipment. Fresh tomatoes or fresh fruit may be used to garnish if available.

8 eggs
¼ pound Cheddar cheese
1 can Vienna sausage
⅛ pound butter

• Chop cheese into small bits. Slice Vienna sausages crosswise into ¼-inch slices. • Break eggs into a large dish and beat. Stir in cheese and sausages. • Melt butter in large frying pan, coating the bottom and sides. Pour egg mixture into pan and prepare as you would scrambled eggs. Salt and pepper to taste before removing from pan.

John K. Northrop

John Northrop and the Flying Wing.

John Northrop was an engineer with an idea—to build planes that were simple and clean in design. His innovative aircraft include the Vega, flown by Wiley Post, Amelia Earhart, and Roscoe Turner; the Alpha, which was a prototype for modern planes with its all-metal stressed skin structure; and the Flying Wing, a tailless turbojet bomber. Previously, planes were designed with little consideration for aerodynamic efficiency, and a number of elements actually added drag. Of his work, Northrop says: "Right from the start, I was interested in making the airplanes efficient aerodynamically. That carried right through my whole life as an airplane designer. I could see the whole world waiting for a plane that was just a little better, a little more efficient, than the planes of that time."* *Recipe and comments from John K. Northrop*

Cottage Cheese Pancakes   Makes 12 medium-size cakes

3 large eggs
¾ cup small curd cottage cheese
¼ cup flour
2 or 3 tablespoons milk
a dash of salt

These should be served in pairs, hot off the pan. If larger quantities are desired, make additional separate batches, as the only leavening is the air entrapped in the egg whites, which gradually escapes. Serve with soft butter or margarine, and syrup or jam; crisp bacon or small grilled sausages also go well. Surprisingly, there is no cottage cheese flavor. The cakes themselves are high protein.

• Separate eggs. Beat yolks to a lemon yellow color. Mix in cottage cheese, flour, salt, and 2 or 3 tablespoons of milk, depending on the thickness desired in the resulting cakes. • Beat egg whites to peaks and gently fold in the batter. • Bake in a nonstick pan, 350° to 375°, or in an electric skillet using a minimum of vegetable oil. Due to the tender consistency, when turning cakes flip in one swift motion as the usual method of using two or three short motions results in torn or broken cakes.

---

*From *Getting off the Ground* by G. Vecsey and G. Dade (New York: E. P. Dutton, 1979)

Paul Poberezny

During half a century of flying, Paul Poberezny's career has involved him in civilian and military aviation as well as the design and development of various homebuilt aircraft, including the popular PoberSport and EEA Acrosport. A high school teacher gave him a glider in 1937 and from that point, he was on his way up. He started his own aircraft maintenance shop after World War II, returning to the Air Force for an eighteen-month tour of Korea. He founded the Experimental Aircraft Association (EEA) in 1953, an organization for hobby flying which sponsors the annual Oshkosh Fly-In. In 1970, when Poberezny resigned from the military, he had the rare distinction of holding seven wings: glider pilot, service pilot, rated pilot, liaison pilot, senior pilot, army aviator, and command pilot. In 1978, the EEA board of directors and the EEA Air Museum Foundation trustees renamed the museum at Franklin, Wisconsin, The Paul H. Poberezny Air Museum in recognition of his lifetime devotion to the improvement of aviation. *Recipe from Paul Poberezny*

No-Peep Chicken   Serves 4

1 chicken, cut in serving pieces
1 cup rice
1 can cream of mushroom soup
1 can cream of chicken soup
1 can cream of celery soup
1 soup can of water
1 envelope dry onion soup

• Butter a 9 × 13-inch pan. Spread rice evenly on the bottom. Arrange pieces of chicken over rice. • Mix the three soups with the water and dry soup mix. Pour over the chicken. • Seal top of pan with foil and bake, without peeping, for 1½ hours at 350°.

Dawson Ransome

Upon receiving his pilot's license at age 16, Dawson Ransome decided to fly all the bridges in Philadelphia—he flew under them, that is. During World War II, he spent a short time as a civilian contract pilot for the Royal Canadian Air Force; he later joined the United States Air Transport Command as a ferry pilot, flying the Asian supply route "hump." After the war, Ransome and his wife Maryann spent weekends restoring and building aircraft, and he was able to continue his early interest in aerobatics by flying his Pitts Special in exhibitions and with the Aerobatic Club of America. He is the founder and president of Ransome Airlines, one of the first companies to offer regular intercity commuter flights in 1967. *Recipes from Mrs. Dawson Ransome*

Bran Muffins   Makes 10

1 cup 100% stone-ground whole wheat flour
1 teaspoon baking soda
1½ cups bran
½ cup raisins
1 egg well beaten
½ cup honey
¾ cup milk
2 tablespoons soft butter

● Mix together dry ingredients and raisins. Moisten with egg, honey, milk, and butter. Stir only to blend. ● Bake in greased muffin tins at 400° for 20 to 30 minutes, or until nicely browned.

Banana-Nut Bread

Makes 1 loaf

½ cup butter
½ cup honey
2 eggs
2¼ cups whole wheat flour
1 cup bran
2 teaspoons baking powder

½ cup milk with 1
   tablespoon vinegar and
   ¼ teaspoon baking soda
1 cup chopped pecans
1 cup mashed bananas
½ teaspoon vanilla

• Cream butter and honey. Add eggs, one at a time, beating well after each addition. • Mix flour, bran, baking powder together. Add flour to butter mixture alternately with milk mixture. • Add mashed bananas, vanilla, and nuts. • Line the bottom of a 9 × 5 × 3-inch loaf pan with waxed paper and grease the bottom and sides well. Bake for 1 hour and 40 minutes at 325°, or until knife inserted in center comes out clean.

Dawson Ransome with his Pitts Special.

Francis M. Rogallo

A love of kite-flying and experience in aerodynamic research led Francis Rogallo to the development of the membrane lifting surface known as the Rogallo Wing. Conceived by Rogallo before 1948 in the course of a private research project, he later applied it to his work on the space program in wind-tunnel research at the Langley Research Center. Although never used for space flight, the wing was adopted by private industry for use as a glider and the sport of hang-gliding came into being. *Recipes and comments from Francis M. Rogallo*

Deviled Crabs

Serves 6

After my retirement from NASA, we moved to Kitty Hawk, North Carolina. Here we devote many happy hours to the catching, preparing, and eating of crabs, but seldom when the wind is just right for gliding on the big dunes. I'll bet it was much the same way at the beginning of the century when the Wright brothers were here.

6 crab shells or ramekins
1 pound crab meat
5 tablespoons butter
1½ tablespoons flour
¾ cup half-and-half
2 eggs, beaten

½ teaspoon salt
1½ teaspoons prepared mustard
½ teaspoon paprika
⅛ teaspoon cayenne pepper

• If using crab shells, wash them well; flake crab meat and remove any cartilage. • Melt 1 tablespoon butter in a saucepan. Stir in flour, then half-and-half and cook, stirring until thick. Remove from heat. • Add eggs, salt, mustard, paprika, and cayenne. Stir. Add crab meat and mix well. • Pack into shells or ramekins. Melt remaining butter and pour over filled shells. Brown quickly under broiler or in a 400° oven.

My wife Gertrude bakes many kinds of pie, but my favorite is this combination of raisins, pecans, and coconut. My liking for raisins in any form I attribute to my early life in Fresno County where raisins played such a dominant role that 'Raisin Day' was our biggest annual festival. I played trumpet in the Sanger band that marched through Fresno as part of the floats, bands, and everything else that makes up a big parade. My two claims to fame are that the girl pictured on the Sun-Maid raisin box was my baby sitter, and that years later I shook the hand of Orville Wright.

Raisin-Nut Pie   Makes 2 9-inch pies

½ cup butter
2 cups sugar
4 eggs
2 teaspoons vanilla
1 teaspoon vinegar
1 cup chopped nuts
1 cup shredded coconut
1 cup raisins
2 9-inch unbaked pie shells

• Preheat oven to 350°. • Cream together butter and sugar. Beat in eggs one at a time, then stir in vanilla and vinegar. • Add nuts, coconut, and raisins. Mix well and pour into unbaked pie shells. • Bake 40 to 45 minutes, or until center is firm. Cooled pie may be wrapped and frozen.

From the dunes of Kitty Hawk, North Carolina, Francis Rogallo takes off in his hang-glider.

Lee R. Scherer

Lee Scherer was the director of the National Aeronautics and Space Administration's Flight Research Center at Edwards Air Force Base in California from 1971 to 1973, and was responsible for the conduct of some of this country's most advanced high-speed aeronautical research. In 1962 he was program manager for Lunar Orbiter, and from 1967 to 1971 was director of the Lunar Exploration Office for Project Apollo. He held this position during the first five manned lunar-landing missions. From 1974 to 1979 he was director of the Kennedy Space Center in Florida. Scherer is now in private industry as vice president for energy services of Stottler, Stagg, and Associates of Cape Canaveral, Florida. *Recipe and comments from Lee R. Scherer*

Magic Cookie Bars   Makes 24 bars

This is so simple that even a klutz like me can bake it with ease. Be advised, however, that the pieces should be cut very small or else the number of calories will be very large!

½ cup butter or margarine, melted
1½ cups graham cracker crumbs
14-ounce can sweetened condensed milk
6-ounce package semisweet chocolate morsels
3⅓-ounce can flaked coconut
1 cup chopped nuts

• Preheat oven to 325°. • Pour melted butter or margarine into a 9 × 13-inch glass baking pan, coating bottom and sides thoroughly. • Sprinkle crumbs over bottom of pan. Pour milk evenly over crumbs. Top with remaining ingredients. • Bake for 25 to 30 minutes, or until lightly browned. Cool completely and cut into bars.

Robert Seamans

A leading authority in the fields of aeronautics and launch vehicles, Robert Seamans was "general manager" of the National Aeronautics and Space Administration from 1960 to 1968. In the role of associate administrator and deputy administrator of NASA, the research, development, and operational base which produced the Apollo lunar-landing program was organized. He was then appointed secretary of the Air Force; and from 1975 to 1977 was administrator of the Energy Research and Development Administration. He is now a visiting professor at the Massachusetts Institute of Technology. *Recipe from Robert Seamans*

Café Brûlot   Serves 8

1 stick of cinnamon
10 whole cloves
1 teaspoon of dried orange peel or the peel of one orange
12 lumps of sugar
1 cup cognac or brandy
4 tablespoons instant regular or decaffeinated coffee
4 cups boiling water

• Break cinnamon into 3 or 4 pieces. Combine in a large covered jar with cloves, peel, sugar, and brandy 4 to 6 hours before using, to allow flavors to mix. • When ready to serve, warm jar gently in hot water. Add boiling water to coffee and put in a hot pot. • Warm a brûlot bowl with boiling water. Pour off water, dry hot bowl, add warm brandy mixture, and ignite. Let it burn about a minute while stirring. • Add hot coffee. Serve at once in demitasse cups.

Robert Six

Currently chairman of the board of Continental Airlines, Inc., Robert Six has worked in the airline business since 1936. At that time, he bought into a small airline company operating one round trip per day between El Paso and Pueblo with three single-engine Lockheed Vegas. In 1937, Six and all sixteen company employees moved to Denver with three twin-engine Lodestars and formed Continental Airlines. The company, presently based in Los Angeles, now has routes that circle half the globe. *Recipe from Robert Six*

Picadillo à la Six

Serves 6

2 pounds lean round steak, ground
½ cup olive oil
2 medium onions, diced
2¾ cups pizza sauce
¾ cup tomato puree or sauce
¾ cup whole canned tomatoes, well drained and diced

1 large sweet pepper, diced
3 garlic cloves, diced
⅓ cup white vinegar
½ teaspoon oregano
cayenne pepper
salt to taste
⅓ cup stuffed manzanilla olives
1 cup dark seedless raisins
1 small bottle capers

• Heat the oil in a heavy skillet. Crumble the ground beef coarsely and add to hot oil. Stir until the meat has changed color, but is not brown. Add the onions to the meat and allow to simmer for a few minutes. • Transfer to a casserole. Add remaining ingredients except the olives, raisins, and capers. Let simmer on low heat for 1 hour, stirring occasionally. Remove any excess fat which may accumulate. • Add the olives, raisins, and capers after other ingredients have cooked 40 minutes. Season to taste with salt and pepper. • Serve over rice or in pita bread.

Richard L. Uppstrom

Colonel Uppstrom is currently the director of the United States Air Force Museum at Wright-Patterson Air Force Base in Ohio, where the collection spans the history of flight from the Wright brothers through the aerospace age. After a varied military career, he is now able to indulge his avid lifetime interest in aviation history. *Recipe and comments from Richard L. Uppstrom*

Quiche Alsace Lorraine   Serves 4

Pie Shell

1¼ cups sifted flour

½ cup grated Parmesan or Cheddar cheese

4 tablespoons chilled butter, cut into pieces

¼ teaspoon salt

4 or 5 tablespoons cold water

I wish I could say that this recipe was captured while on a tour in Europe, but alas the Air Force seems to have made me a specialist in the blue Pacific. The preparation has been done by the wife, and I have specialized in the consumption mode of the partnership. As a nontechnical observer, I'd guess that the filling can be varied to accept almost anything one might find in the larder that catches the palate. Goes well with gin over ice. That is my part of the act.

• Mix flour, cheese, and salt. Cut butter into mixture until the consistency of coarse meal. • Add cold water and stir with a fork. Add additional water if necessary, a drop at a time, until a smooth but not sticky ball of dough is formed. Wrap securely in wax paper and chill at least 1 hour. • Roll out dough and arrange in a 9-inch pie or quiche pan. Place in a 400° oven and partially bake for 10 minutes.

Quiche Filling

½ pound of bacon	1 tablespoon chopped
2 onions, chopped	chives
3 eggs	½ teaspoon salt
1 cup sour cream	¼ teaspoon black pepper
1 cup half-and-half	2 teaspoons caraway seeds

• Preheat oven to 350°. • Cut bacon into small pieces, and fry in a skillet until crisp. Remove and drain on paper towels and set aside. Sauté onions 5 to 10 minutes in remaining fat. • Lightly beat eggs with a wire whisk. Add sour cream, half-and-half, chives, salt, and pepper. Blend until smooth. Add bacon, onions, and mix well. • Carefully pour filling mixture into prebaked pie shell. Sprinkle with caraway seeds. Bake in preheated 350° oven on center shelf, for 30 to 40 minutes, or until top is puffed up and browned and knife inserted into center of custard comes out clean. • Remove from oven onto wire rack for 5 to 10 minutes.

Walter C. Williams

Walter Williams began his career as a junior engineer with the National Advisory Committee on Aeronautics in 1940. In 1946 he was placed in charge of all NACA and National Aeronautics and Space Administration flight-testing activities at Muroc Air Force Base (later renamed Edwards) in California, during which time the first manned supersonic flight was successfully performed. Williams was operations director of Project Mercury, and later associate director of the Manned Spacecraft Center in Houston (now the Johnson Space Center). He joined private industry as a vice president of the Aerospace Corporation in 1964, returning to NASA in 1975 as chief engineer, making assessments of all NASA programs to assure technical excellence. *Recipes from Walter C. Williams*

Hamburger Chili Rellenos   Serves 6

2 pounds ground beef
2 teaspoons salt
pinch black pepper
⅓ cup port wine
1 large onion, chopped fine

1 egg
6 strips green chili
6 ¼ inch strips Monterey
   Jack cheese

● Season ground beef with salt and pepper. Add port wine, chopped onion, and egg. ● Form into six large meatballs. Stuff each meatball with a green chili strip wrapped around a strip of the cheese. Make sure stuffing is secure, then flatten meatballs. ● Fry for 4 or 5 minutes on each side, or longer for well done. ● Serve with refried beans, warmed tortillas with butter, and sliced tomatoes dressed with salt, pepper, and oregano.

Crab Meat Sauté   Serves 2

12 ounces lump or
   regular crabmeat
1 tablespoon butter

1 egg
1 teaspoon Dijon mustard
Worcestershire sauce to taste

● Melt butter in a skillet and sauté the crab meat until it is warm. Break in egg, and add mustard and Worcestershire sauce. Stir until heated and egg is scrambled. ● Serve on toast points.

FOOD IN SPACE

Most people are familiar with airline meals—usually pre-packaged, reheated foods necessitated by the problems of preparing and eating food in flight. The problems of earth-flight eating are minimal, however, in comparison with those of space.

John Glenn became the first American to eat in outer space eighteen years ago, and at that time it was not known if ingestion and absorption of nutrients were possible in a state of zero gravity. Glenn's consumption of applesauce puree and xylose sugar tablets with water proved that dining in space was possible, although far from elegant. The difficulty was not eating or digesting the food, but handling and packaging it for space flight and a weightless environment.

Without gravity, any force applied to an object sends it flying away, and even attempting to convey a simple spoonful of soup to the mouth or stirring ingredients together is impossible. Also, the astronauts' rations had to be compact and require no preparation time that would interfere with their work. Thus, early space meals consisted of pureed food packed into tubes and sucked through a straw in a small opening of the astronauts' helmets. Without the perception of texture or smell, these meals had little to offer except staving off hunger. Changes in suit design which allowed them to remove their helmets inside the spacecraft also meant that bite-size cubes of compressed, dehydrated foods could be eaten, from brownies and chicken sandwiches to "strawberry cereal cubes," coated with gelatin or oil to prevent crumbling. Washed down with water, this basic sustenance was still no gourmet treat.

Dried foods that could be taken into space and rehydrated with hot water were introduced on the Gemini missions, but were still served in pouches. It was not until Apollo 8 that meals were developed that could be eaten with a spoon, in the form of foods that were sticky enough to adhere to their container and to each other. On this Christmas flight a dinner of turkey and gravy with cranberry sauce was served. Bread was prepackaged in a nitrogen atmosphere for long shelf life, and peanut butter and jelly were provided to go with it. Beverages such as lemonade and cocoa made a debut, mixed from powders—but no coffee or tea. Other items such as cookies were developed that were edible in space without first being compressed into dehydrated cubes.

Skylab meals took on more variety. The astronauts chose their own menus, and foods could be heated in their containers, rather than just by the addition of hot water. The chili served proved to be quite troublesome, however, for it tended to explode out of it's package when opened. On the Apollo-Soyuz mission, the Soviet cosmonauts ate tubes of borscht and caviar, dried fish, and small loaves of pumpernickel bread which they shared with the American astronauts.

Space-shuttle meals will be tame by comparison, made up of containers of single-serving, precooked food modules that snap into heating and serving trays. Research now being done focuses not only on how to send food into space, but also on how to create it there. One thing is certain—whether food is grown on a space station in an imitation of earth agriculture, or created synthetically, meals in space will never be the same as Mom's home cooking!

INDEX